WHAT

Rodrigo is a leader in the area of the energetic body, and clairvoyance. This book is a treasure trove of methods that you can use to refine your own powers of perception.
Dr. Peter Fenwick, BA, MB, BChir, DPM, FRCPsych, Consultant Neuropsychiatrist emeritus, Maudsley Hospital, London, UK; Emeritus Senior Lecturer, Institute of Psychiatry, London, UK; Co-author (with Elizabeth Fenwick) of *The Art of Dying*

A well thought out guidebook for the practice of visual clairvoyance.
Robert Bruce, author of *Astral Dynamics*

In recent years, "clairvoyance" and "remote viewing" have received considerable attention in both the parapsychological literature and the popular media. In this provocative book, Rodrigo Medeiros presents step-by-step instructions to develop visual clairvoyance as a vehicle for spiritual evolution. Some readers will find this procedure too esoteric, but others will discover a personal discipline that will enrich their lives and uncover new dimensions of experience.
Stanley Krippner, Ph.D., Co-author *Personal Mythology*

Paravision represents an exceptional contribution to existing understanding of this fascinating phenomenon, explaining in depth, and from a scientific perspective, the mechanisms that give rise to it. With over 20 years' experience in teaching conscientiology, over 15 years' researching paravision, and a wealth of personal experience, Rodrigo's expertise allows us to understand paravision, to experience it ourselves, and to harness its power as a tool for personal evolution.

Sandie Gustus, author, *Less Incomplete: A Guide to Experiencing the Human Condition beyond the Physical Body*

Paravision

Theory and Practice of
Visual Clairvoyance

Paravision

Theory and Practice of
Visual Clairvoyance

Rodrigo Medeiros

Winchester, UK
Washington, USA

First published by Sixth Books, 2018
Sixth Books is an imprint of John Hunt Publishing Ltd., Laurel House, Station Approach,
Alresford, Hants, SO24 9JH, UK
office1@jhpbooks.net
www.johnhuntpublishing.com
www.6th-books.com

For distributor details and how to order please visit the 'Ordering' section on our website.

Text copyright: Rodrigo Medeiros 2016

ISBN: 978 1 78535 132 7
978 1 78535 564 6 (ebook)
Library of Congress Control Number: 2016957605

A CIP catalogue record for this book is available from the British Library.

Design: Stuart Davies

Printed and bound by CPI Group (UK) Ltd, Croydon, CR0 4YY, UK

We operate a distinctive and ethical publishing philosophy in all
areas of our business, from our global network of authors to
production and worldwide distribution.

CONTENTS

Introduction

On that day, clairvoyance started spontaneously. Right at the start of the exercise I could clearly see the energetic dimension as a type of fog starting about five feet from me and that filled the whole room. After one hour into the technique I noticed the contour of three extraphysical consciousnesses (spirits) to my right, close to my feet. I saw oval shapes only initially, an outline defined by a bright line that delineated their energy field. The outlines of the two of them fused from time to time, perhaps due to their proximity, or due to an energetic connection between them.

I focused on those outlines and tried to see the face and more detail from those presences, then started to see bright spots in the upper region of the oval outline. I knew that this perception indicated the position of the head of a non-physical being.

I tried to connect energetically to those consciousnesses to facilitate clairvoyance, which allowed me to perceive a pattern of energy that was very calm, yet determined, a mix of concentration and serenity, hard to describe.

I was reclined in the chair and noticed that one of the three started to move, as if gliding, going around the recliner and stopping close to my head, where I clearly perceived her energetic presence. I then felt the activation of my coronochakra, as if a hot ring was placed on top of my head.

The two other consciousnesses also moved and stopped about ten inches from each of my feet. At this point I was able to see more detail of the extraphysical consciousness to my right, as if the surface of her psychosoma [astral body] became semitransparent, allowing me to identify a feminine face, with straight shoulder-length hair. All three started to exteriorize energies towards me until it triggered a vibrational state. I could feel my whole energy body vibrating intensely, a pleasant sensation that lasted several minutes [...]

1

Paravision: A Natural Phenomenon

This book explores one of the richest parapsychic capacities of all – paravision. There are countless references to this phenomenon in history, mystic literature, and popular culture. However, the approach used in this book tries to be both practical and technical, so that this skill can be put to good use and to promote personal growth.

Paravision is a form of visual perception beyond our physical eyes. It is a type of psychic ability that allows us to see auras, non-physical energies, non-physical dimensions, and more. The main objectives of this book are to explain how this phenomenon works, to present techniques for you to experience it, and to present ideas on how it connects to personal growth.

The account you have just read shows how clairvoyance allows a greater, deeper, and closer participation in events that include elements beyond the physical dimension.

The experience above includes a variety of perceptions: the sensation of extraphysical presences, the movement of those presences, the perception of a serene pattern of energies, the activation of chakras, and the vibrational state. Each perception was very interesting in isolation. With paravision, however, I was able to add a visual element to the experience that allowed me to put the other perceptions into context. Paravision allowed me to "connect the dots" and understand what was happening around me, in other dimensions. This makes a world of difference in terms of learning and personal growth.

Clairvoyance and Paravision

The term *Clairvoyance* has different meanings depending on the line of study and period in history where it is used. Sometimes it has a **broad** meaning and is defined as *any* ability to interact with non-physical dimensions. Sometimes clairvoyance is presented with more **specific** meaning, as the ability to see auras, spirits, and energies.

The approach adopted in this book follows the conscienti-ology paradigm (more on that later). In this paradigm, the terms "paravision" and "clairvoyance" are interchangeable, and mean specifically perceiving *images* from non-physical dimensions, images that cannot be seen with the physical eyes.

I will use the term "parapsychism" for the broad sense of the word clairvoyance, meaning *any* type of non-physical perception. Examples of parapsychism include reading infor-mation from a personal object (psychometry) and receiving a thought from someone else beyond physical means (telepathy).

Visual Perception and Psychic Ability

Physical visual perception is very interesting, a key part of our existence. Some researchers argue that as much as eighty percent of the total of our perception is visual. Forms and images have a strong presence in our lives. When we choose clothes, furniture, houses, cars, and other objects it is hard to ignore the allure of physical appearance. Marketing strategies constantly try to exploit the visual appeal of products.

The richness of visual perception may be the reason why people talk more about the design of a new car than about non-visual sensations associated to it. The smell, engine noise, sensation when touching the steering wheel, or even the practical aspects related to the central function of a car – a means of locomotion – often become secondary when talking about an automobile.

There are numerous expressions that show the importance of visual perception in our everyday life, "seeing is believing," and "a picture is worth a thousand words," for example.

Since clairvoyance is a form of *visual* perception, we can say that developing this ability is, at the very least, stimulating, because if combines the richness of visual perception with the infinite possibilities of bioenergies and dimensions beyond the physical world.

To open your "eyes" to what lies beyond the physical dimension also means to participate more directly in what is already happening around you in those other dimensions. Those events typically go undetected, since you cannot perceive them with the physical senses.

The Disbelief Principle

A central hypothesis in this book is that clairvoyance allows you to see things that are not physical, through a type of visual perception that is independent from physical light, physical eyes, and overall physical body.

It is not my objective to *convince* or *prove* that clairvoyance exists and can be developed. The proposition is for the reader to acquire a theoretical basis, apply practical techniques, seek personal experiences with clairvoyance, and later analyze the results with openness, questioning, and logical reasoning. With that, the reader can reach his or her own conclusions.

This proposition is embodied in a sentence often seen in places where conscientiology is taught and discussed:

Do not believe in anything, not even what you are reading in this book.

Experiment, have your own experiences.

Clairvoyance is an ambivalent phenomenon, as it is the case with physical vision. We cannot "get inside of someone's head" to see how she sees the world. It is necessary to ask this person to describe her perceptions. We can create experiments and develop language to deepen our knowledge about the phenomenon, but we will always depend on the description of those who have personal experiences. And, of course, those descriptions can have varying levels of objectivity and detail.

As it is the case in several types of psychic perception, the accumulation of experiences helps to identify the difference between clairvoyance and other visual phenomena.

Structure
This book is organized in three parts:

1. **Fundamental concepts**, chapters 1 to 3;
2. **Clairvoyance concepts**, chapters 4, 5, 6, and 9
3. **Techniques**, chapters 7 and 8.

The second part of the book is intended to help in the clairvoyance development, although it does not include step-by-step instructions or techniques per se. We recommend that you read that section for two reasons.

First, because when you know the phenomenon in more detail – what it is, what it is not, and how it works – it will be easier to develop it. Second, because you will find – within the examples and anecdotes experienced by the author and others – tips and information to better understand and apply the techniques described in part three.

For those who know something about the topic: it is important to highlight that even in the explanation of fundamental concepts such as bioenergy, out-of-body experience, and other phenomena, you will find information that can help in clairvoyance development. You will see examples and accounts embedded in those explanations that can help you see specific aspects of parapsychism from a different angle. Exploring different angles of the phenomenon has a great potential to increase the repertoire of perceptions during your experiments with extraphysical vision.

Theoretical-Practical Basis
The definitions and general understanding of the parapsychic phenomena presented here are based on conscientiology, a

science that studies consciousness and its evolution. Paraperceptiology and projectiology are the specialties more directly connected to the phenomena addressed here, as we will later see. Conscientiology, and its 300 specialties, is a science proposed by the independent researcher Waldo Vieira (1932 – 2015).

Some of the techniques and explanations utilized here come from courses in conscientiology or are derived from my experience and twenty years of teaching curricular courses as a volunteer in conscientiology-related organizations.

The influence of several instructors who work in and lead the organizations that develop conscientiology is evident in this book and relevant to the book. Such influence, in a way, broadens and strengthens the so-called "consensus among researchers," a necessity generally referenced in conscientiological texts.

More specifically, the text aims at sharing techniques, data collected, and theories developed during the presentation of two courses I have created: "Developing your Clairvoyance" and "Clairvoyance Workshop." These courses have been given in the US (Miami, New York, Los Angeles, Houston, Gainesville, Delray Beach, Austin); China (Hong Kong, Macau); Finland (Helsinki); Spain (Madrid, Barcelona, Seville); Sweden (Stockholm); Portugal (Lisbon, Porto); Italy (Bergamo, Milan); Mexico (Mexico City); Netherlands (Rotterdam, Zutphen); and the UK (London, Devon).

The analysis of the parapsychic experiments (my own and of participants) carried out during these courses have guided several of the approaches discussed in these pages. Names of colleagues, students in the workshops, and participants in events in general were changed, as some of these accounts may contain information considered personal.

Motivation and Origin of this Research

I started to study themes related to parapsychism motivated

mainly by curiosity. I was also a bit of a non-conformist in regards to the "life options" that, apparently, most people around me were looking to fit in. I was skeptical about the general formula where I would study, then get a job, earn a living, get married, have kids, enjoy the weekends and holidays, then retire and later die. I felt that there was something missing in this proposition, the logic seemed incomplete. Is there anything beyond this? The idea of heaven and hell seemed absurd to me.

One day, a friend with whom I would talk about things considered "beyond normal," like invisible energies and beings from other dimensions, mentioned "this institute" where we could attend a lecture about out-of-body experiences and related topics.

I attended a free lecture, thought the approach was interesting and started to participate in courses. I then learned to work with energies and to apply techniques to induce out-of-body experiences. After some time, I became a volunteer and conscientiology instructor, initially teaching in Brazil and, later, in several cities in the United States, Mexico, and Europe.

I developed clairvoyance and other forms of parapsychism through techniques, self-experimentation, and will power.

Patricia Sousa – a researcher and instructor of conscientiology – and I created the research project "Image Target," which generated interesting data about differences between observing an image through an OBE or Remote Viewing. The results of this research were presented in the III ICPC – International Congress of Conscientiology and Projectiology.

The experience with dozens of clairvoyance workshops highlighted the motivating aspect that a first-hand experience can have. It is one thing to read or hear about clairvoyance, something that, of course, has its benefits – better to know than to ignore. However, what really makes one understand the multidimensional reality in which we are inserted in is to see, first hand, with one's own *para*eyes.

Objectives

The central idea of this book is to present a technical approach to clairvoyance, one that is neither mystical nor religious, with the central goal being personal development (evolution).

Clairvoyance is the phenomenon of visual perception of *extra-physical* realities, in the present. This is the ability that allows us to see the aura, non-physical energies from another person, and non-physical events.

As presented earlier, the term "clairvoyance" had many meanings throughout history. Even today the exact meaning depends on which author or theoretical base selected. For clarity, the definition of clairvoyance use throughout this book has three main characteristics:

1. It is *extra*physical, or beyond the physical dimension.
2. It is visual, and not auditory or tactile, for instance.
3. It is a perception of the *now*, of the present, and not a memory or premonition.

Clairvoyance can be divided into two types depending on the distance between the experimenter and the observed target: *local clairvoyance* and *travelling clairvoyance.*

Local clairvoyance (LC) means using clairvoyance to see something in your immediate environment. An example of local clairvoyance would be you seeing the aura of a work colleague during a meeting in which both of you are in the same physical location.

Travelling clairvoyance (TC) is the skill used to see something that is happening at a distance. For example, you are in London and you see something that is happening in Buenos Aires. Travelling clairvoyance became a popular topic in the 1970s and 1980s and it more commonly known as "remote viewing."

Exploring Local Clairvoyance

Although we will see examples of both local and travelling clairvoyance in the next few chapters, the focus will be on local clairvoyance.

There are several practical reasons for this. First, local clairvoyance development is easier, generally speaking, for those who are starting.

Second, travelling clairvoyance requires more knowledge and attention to be differentiated from phenomena such as the hypnagogic state and out-of-body experience, as we will discuss in the chapter "Clairvoyance and other Phenomena."

Third, travelling clairvoyance requires a deeper altered state of consciousness when compared to local clairvoyance. As such, TC usually requires a bit more practice and training in order to master the necessary altered state to produce the phenomenon.

Fourth, local clairvoyance can be experienced with open eyes and without hard-to-acquire technical abilities. Because experiments can be done with your eyes open, the distinction between clairvoyance and imagination, or oneiric images is facilitated. It is also easier to stay in control and avoid entering deeper and more complex altered states of consciousness, which could make the interpretation of the experience a bit harder.

Accessible Language

Another objective of this book is to present information that may help readers understand their own parapsychic experiences related to visual perception. Various types of visual perception will be presented and compared. Several accounts from workshops, from people with various backgrounds will be presented in order to illustrate the possibilities of clairvoyance.

Some technical aspects of physical and extraphysical are not necessarily simple. This book is, however, an attempt to present information in a technical manner, giving priority to information that helps in clairvoyance development.

The aim is also to explain with didactic clarity, without simplifying what cannot be simplified, but at the same time without complicating what is intrinsically simple. Aspects that had little or no practical application were omitted. The book presents references in certain topics for those who wish to go deeper where a limited explanation was provided.

Some conscientiology themes are presented in a brief and objective manner, limiting the scope to what is essential to understand a certain concept and its relation to clairvoyance. For more detail on such topics, please consult the section "Conscientiological Bibliography."

In some paragraphs I used his and her instead of his/her, with the intention of having a more fluid text. In those instances, the reference applies to both genders.

Presenting Techniques and Exercises

To read and understand theory always helps when we are trying to develop any ability. However, as any swimming instructor would say, "at some point you have to dive in and start swimming."

When talking theory, most people want to see techniques and step-by-step instructions that quickly produce results. While there is nothing wrong in trying to find the shortest path that will lead to experiences, I would keep in mind that techniques and step-by-step instructions are less effective – and sometimes not effective at all – when applied without a theoretical base that helps you to understand the phenomenon.

This is why most techniques are presented later in this book. I recommend that the theoretical part to be read first so you are better prepared to benefit from techniques.

Some techniques are meant for those who are starting and do not have any experience or practice. Other techniques will work better if you have already accumulated some experience with extraphysical vision. Regardless of where you are in terms of development, all techniques can help you develop better control of the phenomenon and to explore new aspects of your extra-physical perception.

Learn How to Switch It on and "Change Channels"

There are two skills that can help you in the development of your clairvoyance. The first is to learn how to "switch it on" and start seeing nonphysical things, a process described in Chapter 6, in the section "Finding the Switch." This part is relatively easy and takes time measured in hours and days if you apply the right techniques.

The second one involves changing the target dimension, something roughly equivalent to changing channels on the TV. I call this process changing the "clairvoyance tuning." This process is most important to sustain the development of your extraphysical vision, because you learn how to control your clair-voyance and direct it at will. This process is described in Chapter 4, in the section "Dimensional Tuning." The time to develop this ability varies more, from hours to months, depending on the experimenter's profile and the techniques applied, but can bring the most interesting types of perception.

Anti-Indoctrination

This book does not seek to disseminate fixed, immutable ideas, or some sort of doctrine, old or new. Quite to the contrary, the goal is to present a version of what is understood about clair-voyance using a specific paradigm. It is expected that future editions of this book will change some of the theories and techniques, as we investigate, learn and discover more about clairvoyance.

Leading Edge Relative Truth

The term used in conscientiology to describe the most up-to-date knowledge that is consensus among researchers is *leading edge relative truth.* "Leading edge" because it is the most recent, *avant-garde*, the best theory up until now, or a relative consensus among researchers and experimenters. "Relative" because it can change as we discover more about the subject.

The classification of phenomena we will explore may not align with what you have read from other philosophies, religions or mystical approaches. The intention to reclassify, regroup and redefine is to understand the phenomena with more clarity and precision, based on what we know at this moment.

New Words

In some cases, terms used to identify aspects relative to clairvoyance are different from more popular terms. For example, we will use "energosoma" instead of "etheric body," with the objective of having a single, clear definition, and in order to have uniformity across the names of our multiple bodies (energo, for energy + soma, for body). Those new words are *neologisms* and will not be found in a common dictionary at this point.

A new term often helps to establish a more precise definition of a phenomenon, especially when older terms have been defined in different ways or with less precision throughout history.

In some cases, the popular or traditional term is used for lack of a better expression or because no better term is available yet. For instance, "silver cord," the connection between the physical body and our astral body (psychosoma), is not made of silver, is not always seen as silver (color), and does not behave exactly like a cord. We will, however, use this expression in this book, and until a new, better, expression becomes available.

The next chapter will introduce several neologisms as we explore definitions and concepts used throughout this book.

Chapter 1

Basic Definitions

Bioenergies

Bioenergy is synonym of chi, prana, orgone, vital energy, mesmeric fluid, vital fluid, and several additional terms coined throughout history. This is a type of energy that is not physical and it is a different form of energy from, for instance, the chemical energy of gasoline or the energy in electromagnetic radio waves. Gasoline and radio waves are in the physical dimension, bioenergies are *extra*physical.

We have a bioenergy body and interact with others with its energy in our day-to-day life. Most people, however, experience bioenergies indirectly, intuitively, or without a more thorough understanding of its mechanisms and how it works.

Perhaps you have had the following experience: in the first encounter with a certain person, you have the clear feeling that she is positive and trustworthy, even without having concrete evidence or previous experiences that justify your assessment.

This information, which you are sure about, despite being unable to confirm it at that moment (positivity and trustworthiness), can be transmitted through bioenergies. The feeling that you can trust that person may even contradict her physical presentation: she is poorly dressed and speaks with hesitation. The bioenergies, however, convey a stronger message: you can trust her.

On the other hand, sometimes, we get into a place that is aesthetically beautiful, clean, visually amenable, but where we don't feel at ease. We may say that the "atmosphere" is not good, or that it has a "bad vibe," or something strange "in the air," This and many expressions indicate the quality of the energy. In this example, a quality that makes it not desirable or incompatible from your point of view.

Charisma and axé are expressions that point towards bioenergy attributes or to bioenergy itself. The integration of such words into the dictionary of many cultures show the relative popularity of the capacity to perceive and use bioenergies, even when at an unconscious level.

Consciousness

You and I, and all living beings are consciousnesses. The consciousness is not something physical, it is not a body, nor a type of energy. It is, instead, an *intelligent and organizing element* of physical matter and extraphysical energy.

As I write this book, I, a consciousness, transmit ideas through words written on paper. I use my physical body to press keys on the keyboard in my computer and my eyes to verify if I typed the words correctly. After that, the digital version of the book is transformed in printed letters on paper (assuming you are reading this in printed media). The source of the ideas, however, is not by brain, fingers, or eyes. And, clearly, not the letters on paper. The source of the ideas is a consciousness.

I am, therefore, talking about me in a dualist way. I am trying to understand the universe as something made of at least two elements: (1) matter, which composes my physical body and all objects around, and (2) the consciousness, the thinking element, the component trying to transmit ideas through sentences and concepts and words.

The consciousness, therefore, utilizes the brain, the physical body, and the bioenergies to interact with the environment and with other consciousnesses.

This approach is the opposite of the theory that conventional science often tries to convey: that we, consciousness, are a product of the brain. Conscientiology proposes that the brain and other vehicles of manifestation are products originated by a consciousness.

14

Immanent and Consciential Energy

The extraphysical energy can be classified in two basic types. The first one groups bioenergies form the earth, air, and water, for example. This is the **immanent energy**. There are no specific thought or sentiment in this type of energy since it has not been modified by a living being, in other words, it has not been modified by any consciousness.

If you have been on a beach, forest or meadow where not many people go, you probably felt the typical pattern of immanent energy.

In contrast to this scenario, if you have been in a congress for professionals in a specific field, or in a rock band concert, you would have perceived the second type of bioenergies, one that is modified by thoughts and sentiments. This second type of bioenergies is the **consciential energy** and it carries information imprinted by the consciousness. Thoughts and sentiments are examples of information contained in consciential energy.

Thosene and Holothosene

The modification of bioenergies through the manifestation of consciousness will "season" the energies and give it a particular "taste."

If Miriam studies Nietzsche philosophy, thoughts and sentiments related to existential themes will be imprinted in her energies.

Thoughts and emotions accumulate over time in our personal energy field, creating a summary, or weighted average, of our *actions of thinking and feeling*.

If Lucas is often dramatic in his manifestations, thoughts, and interactions, his field of energies will reflect that. Someone that does not know anything about his life could pick up this information by getting in contact with his energies. Due to the strength and frequency of emotions in Lucas's manifestation, energies with a dramatic pattern become part of his "energetic business card."

Thosene (*tho* for thought, *sen* for sentiment + *ene* for energy) is a composite word that means the amalgam of these three elements, which are the basis for our consciential manifestation.

Our manifestation always contains each of the three elements, in varying degrees of intensity. So we would not externalize energies with absolutely no thoughts or sentiments, just as we will not think without modifying our energy with that pattern, or have an emotion without imprinting it in our energies. Each manifestation generates a certain amount of those three elements, depending on the situation.

Thosenes do not dissipate immediately and tend to accumulate, forming *holo*thosenes. People, places, and objects have a holothosene, which is the result of this accumulation over time, synthetized in a type of weighted average, according to the frequency and intensity of thoughts and sentiments generated by the consciousnesses involved.

The main connection of this concept with clairvoyance is that the holothosene determines the pattern of consciousnesses around you, in any dimension. We will go back to this topic in the chapter "Clairvoyance Techniques," when we discuss facial clairvoyance.

In bioenergy language, the holothosene can be read and can be amenable, welcoming, or not, depending on the pattern of the consciousness in contact with this holothosene.

Vehicles of Consciousness

So, if we, consciousness, are not physical, then how do we interact with the environment around us? The answer is that we use vehicles (or bodies) for this. We have a set of bodies called *holosoma* in the context of conscientiology.

The holosoma includes four bodies: soma, energosoma (or holochakra), psychosoma and mentalsoma.

The most dense is the **soma**, the biological, physical,

biochemical body. To keep it functioning well we need to eat, sleep, exercise, and take care of our physical health.

The second body is the **energosoma**, or the bioenergy body. This vehicle is the one that contains the chakras or centers of energy. This is the body that you use to perceive the pattern of bioenergies from a place or from another person.

The energosoma is a vitalizing agent of the physical body and several practices, alternative therapies, and techniques seek to work with this vehicle. Reiki, Chi Kung (or Qi Gong) are examples of such practices.

Because it is slightly bigger than the physical body we see the energosoma as a bright contour enveloping the physical body of the person we are looking at. This is one of the most common clairvoyance perceptions.

The aura is a field or envelope around people, animals, plants, and objects, which can present itself with various colors and varying thickness. In humans, it is normally perceived as a layer with thickness between five and twenty inches, although the aura can at times reach several feet.

The limit of the aura can be visualized through clairvoyance and even perceived with your hands. The sensation can be of a subtle barrier or mild change of temperature that defines the edge of the personal energy field.

Thoughts, sentiments, and energy movement can change the size, color and shape of our aura.

The third body is the **psychosoma**. This vehicle is popularly known as astral body, and known as perispirit in spiritualism. The psychosoma is the vehicle used in an out-of-body experience (or astral projection, OBE). This is the vehicle that allows us to have clairvoyance perceptions.

A lot of people ask if clairvoyance happens through the energosoma or through the psychosoma. Waldo Vieira, in the treatise Projectiology, indicates that the extraphysical clairvoyance happens through the *para*eyes of the psychosoma, meaning, the perception is based on the psychosoma. This hypothesis is reinforced if we consider accounts of visual perceptions of bioenergies and auras by people that have already died, even from those who no longer have an energosoma.

When we are awake and have our eyes open, during the ordinary waking state, clairvoyance is experienced via the psychosoma, not through our physical eyes. We will explore this topic in greater depth later.

The fourth body is the *mentalsoma*, the vehicle of discernment (capacity to choose well). The same way we need the physical body to breathe, we need the mentalsoma to think. This vehicle is probably the most complex of all, being comprised of various attributes (concentration, comprehension, logic, and discernment), and is intimately connected to patterns of thought (ability to set limitations, self-confidence, beliefs, mental conditioning, and self-control).

The mentalsoma has a key role in evolution and in the evaluation of our experiences. This fundamental concept of conscientiology is explored thoroughly in Vieira's *700 Experiments of Conscientiology*. The prioritization of the development and application of the attributes of the mentalsoma is fundamental to the expansion of one's parapsychism in a healthy and productive way.

A mentalsoma projection is a relatively rare phenomenon when compared with the more frequent psychosoma projection. The mentalsoma projection, however, is remarkable to the point of defining a "before and after" point in the experimenter's evolution timeline. It transcends the parameters of everyday life in this dimension and the parameters of time-space through a powerful intellectual expansion. The phenomenon of cosmoconsciousness is also related to this vehicle.

We can have different levels of heath and preparedness of specific attributes of each vehicle. For example, my physical body may be able to cope with running three miles in less than thirty minutes. In order to achieve this, I need certain muscles in my legs and my cardiovascular system to be developed to support this activity.

Likewise, my mentalsoma may be fit so I can maintain a reasonable level of concentration for four hours during a math test.

The mentalsoma is relevant in clairvoyance development to the extent that it can limit our perceptions and manifestations. My mentalsoma could contribute to me being more or less open to perceiving, and more or less prone to incorrectly discard subtle perceptions that I had. We will explore this aspect in many areas of Chapter 6, particularly when we discuss self-blocking.

Consciousness and Its States

A person that is alive and awake has those four bodies available to interact with her surroundings. Because the consciousness is *inside* the physical body, we say that this is an *intraphysical* conscin, or to abbreviate, "conscin" (*consc*, of consciousness + *in* of intraphysical).

Those in a period between this life and the next, in other words, those who died and are not yet *re*born, do not have a physical body that can be used in their manifestation. We call those consciousnesses *extraphysical*. They are real and continue to exist, but we would need some form of parapsychic ability in order to contact them from the physical dimension. To shorten the term for a consciousness that is extraphysical, we use the term conscex (*consc*, of consciousness + *ex*, of extraphysical).

Intraphysical and extraphysical are two of the possible states of consciousness. Intraphysical for the consciousness that is alive and has a physical body, and extraphysical for the conciousness that does not have a physical body, already died, and is currently in the period between lives.

There is also a third consciousness state, the *projected* state. This is when an intraphysical consciousness temporarily leaves the physical body (soma) with the psychosoma, in an out-of-body experience (or astral travel, astral projection).

Non-Alignment of the Vehicles of Manifestation

The vehicles of manifestation we discussed can be at varying degrees of alignment. When we are awake our vehicles are well aligned, engaged, connected. As we relax our physical body, our energies naturally expand, allowing for more space for our psychosoma to move around.

Clairvoyance tends to develop more easily when our vehicles are in slight misaligned. This is why a lot of relaxation techniques include elements to induce relaxation, which in turn will tend to allow for an expansion of our energies and a slight misalignment of the psychosoma.

Dimensions

Thinking in a simplistic way, our bodies need to be in a "place" at any given time. The problem is that my psychosoma, at this moment, as I write, is technically occupying the same "place" as my soma, since I am awake and with the vehicles in alignment. This is where dimensions (or planes) come into it. My psychosoma is in the *extraphysical* dimension, while my soma is in the *physical* dimension. This way both bodies can occupy the same "place" in space, as they are in different dimensions.

There are several analogies used to describe dimensions, and the most common, perhaps, is the one that uses the concept of frequencies and radio waves. In this analogy, we establish a parallel between radio wave frequencies and dimensions, alluding to the fact that radio waves can "occupy" the same space at the same time, with different frequencies.

Each radio station transmits its signal in a specific frequency. For example, station "A" can transmit at 73MHz and station "B" in 75MHz. Both signals reach your car or your home and you need your radio receiver to tune into one station or the other, so you can listen to only one station.

Similarly, the "signal" or "station" of clairvoyance is always present, however most people are "tuned" exclusively into their physical vision, and therefore excluding (or filtering) any perception from other dimensions.

In fact, most people are used to a strong and clear "signal" from the intraphysical dimension, in such a way that any stimuli coming from other dimensions is ignored or received in indirect ways, for example, intuitively.

Another reason why relaxation is an important component of several clairvoyance techniques presented in this book is that it reduces the "signal strength" of the physical dimension. A weaker perceived signal from the physical dimension makes it easier to perceive the signals of the energetic and extraphysical dimensions.

The model of dimensions in conscientiology includes four dimensions: physical, energetic, extraphysical, and mentalsomatic.

We interact with the physical dimension with our soma (physical body). All physical objects, animals, plants, electromagnetic waves, electrostatic fields, and magnetic fields are in this dimension.

Bioenergies, both from our energy body and immanent energies, are in the energetic dimension. You cannot see this dimension with your physical eyes. To have visual perceptions of the energetic dimension you need clairvoyance.

It is relatively common to see the following accounts after a clairvoyance exercise: "It looked like the room was foggy, as if I was inside of a cloud." This is one of the typical perceptions from the energy dimension, which is also known by the name *dimener*.

The perception of the energosoma and of the aura are also visual perceptions of the energy dimension.

When someone sees the psychosoma of an extraphysical consciousness (conscex, spirit, entity) then this perception is from the *extraphysical* dimension. Extraphysical consciousnesses present themselves through the psychosoma, as they no longer have a soma, and the psychosoma is the extraphysical dimension.

The mentalsoma dimension is the extraphysical environment of the mentalsoma. Clairvoyance typically gives access to the energetic and extraphysical dimensions. Non-physical visual perceptions of the mentalsoma dimension fall into the more speculative area, perhaps associated with capturing original extraphysical ideas.

There are several mentalsoma attributes that are useful, and often fundamental, during clairvoyance development. The ability to focus and silence your own thoughts are examples in this category. Most of the work, however, is associated with the soma (physical relaxation) and energosoma (unblocking and looseness).

Some lines of thought, religions and mysticism assign a number to each dimension, calling them first, second, third, and fourth, for example. This can cause a bit of confusion with the parameters length-height-width, which are three *dimensions* in the physical world.

The problem here is in the use of the word *dimension*. "Width" is a dimension, but meaning "direction in which extent is measured." When we say the "energetic dimension," the meaning of the word *dimension* is different. In this context, dimension means "a place in space," extraphysical space in this case, and **not** measurement in a certain direction.

It is possible that in the past the term "fourth dimension" was used as an analogy to explain non-physical dimensions. In this analogy, you could show the first three dimensions, which would be easy to understand in physical terms and easy to verify, say, by examining a wooden cube, and asking the observer to think what the fourth dimension would be. This fourth dimension would go beyond the first three, and would be something "inside" the cube, something beyond the length, height and width.

Other theories, lines of thinking and mysticisms propose seven, ten or fifteen dimensions. At times the concept of altered states of consciousness is mixed in the description of the dimension in those theories, creating a model that can be difficult to grasp.

The model used in conscientiology, however, is based on four dimensions: physical, energetic, extraphysical, and mentalsomatic. This set of four seem suitable to describe the known phenomena up to this point, and will be the model used throughout this book.

Extraphysical and the Prefix "Para"

You have probably noticed by now that I have used the prefix "para" in front of some words. This prefix indicates that the element that comes after it is in an extraphysical dimension. In other words, whatever comes after "para" is not in the physical dimension, it is beyond the physical world. For example, *para*-eyes are the extraphysical eyes of the psychosoma, the *para*-head, the extraphysical head of the psychosoma, *para*-perception is the extraphysical perception, and so on.

Dimensions and Densities

From physics, density is the ration between quantity of matter and volume for a given physical object. We know that a glass of condensed milk is heavier than a glass of regular milk. Considering that the cup is of the same size, i.e., that the volume is the same, we can say that condensed milk is denser than regular milk.

Empirically, we know that Styrofoam is less dense than lead, and that the air is less dense than water, and so on.

The concept of density can also be applied to dimensions and energies in general. Accounts and articles frequently include sentences like "I perceived denser energies," "I arrived in a denser dimension during the OBE," or "I got in contact with an extraphysical consciousness in a more subtle dimension."

From the clairvoyance perspective, a consideration in regards to density is that denser energies are, in general, more easily observed during practical exercises. As such, we will create better conditions to experience clairvoyance if we densify the field of energies around us. We will later discuss exercises such as the exteriorization of energies, which can be used to densify the energies around us.

An extraphysical consciousness that is denser can also be more easily observed, since they are in a dimension that is "closer" to the physical one.

Another observation is that clairvoyance has this "tuning" characteristic, which allows the experimenter to see, selectively, energies with different densities within a dimension. For example, an experimenter can see the energosoma (more dense energy) of another person, and seconds later switch to seeing the energies around her (less dense energy).

The majority of experimenters see the energosoma first or more often, at least in the first attempts. The energies of the surroundings (not associated to a living person), and the outer layers of the aura tend to be less dense. Those less dense areas tend to require a bit more concentration and, sometimes, more patience and determination, to be seen with clarity.

Energetic Coupling

Two consciousnesses can temporarily merge or fuse their energetic fields. This condition, called energetic coupling, makes it easier to exchange thoughts and sentiments imprinted in our energies (thosenes). The energetic coupling happens naturally if the two people have affinity or common interests. Waldo Vieira defines energetic coupling as "a temporary fusion of the auras of two consciousnesses."

The energetic coupling happens naturally during a conversation between friends and intensifies as both engage with more intensity in the exchange of ideas. At times, it can get to the point where you know what the other person is going to say even before she says it because you have already received the information via thosenes.

Due to the facilitated flow of thosenes, mutual comprehension is facilitated during the energy coupling. This makes it easier to understand the context, situation, complex feelings, and insights conveyed, and possibly communicate those ideas with fewer words, since the energies are transmitting a considerable amount of unspoken information.

This kind of coupling can also connect a group of people, which can explain the "group contagion" where several people in a theatre yawn in a short period of time following the first yawn. The group energetic coupling can also, for example, make a comedy funnier when seen in a movie theatre, due to the interaction with the holothosene of the group watching that movie.

Distance does not seem to interfere with such couplings. People separated by thousands of miles can initiate an energetic connection through a phone conversation, internet video chat, or reading a letter or e-mail.

The energetic coupling can also happen between consciounesses in any of the states described before: intraphysical, extraphysical, and projected.

As an example, you, an intraphysical consciousness, can establish an energetic coupling with your neighbor, when both are in the waking state. In a more elaborate scenario, you could establish an energetic coupling while both are projected, in an out of body experience.

Moreover, a connection can be established between an intraphysical consciousness and an extraphysical consciousness. For example, Joana, an intraphysical consciousness, can establish an energetic coupling with her aunt who died a few years before, then feel her presence, her mood, and general pattern of thoughts. This kind of coupling can be established by "evoking the consciousness that is no longer alive." The act of thinking for a while about this person, now in the extraphysical dimension, tend to "call" this consciousness. The efficacy of evoking is proportional to the intensity of thoughts and sentiments related to that person.

This evocation followed by auric coupling can create a vicious cycle: evocation, coupling, remembrance, more evocation. This maintains the conscin in constant contact with the conscex, a process that can delay the adaptation of the conscex to her new condition: a period between lives.

A process like this can also make it harder for the intraphysical consciousness to adapt to her new condition: a temporary separation from the other consciousness. At times, the evocations and energy coupling go on for years and, depending on the involved, can come with painful emotions and suffering.

On another example, a lucid extraphysical consciousness that is able and willing to help can also be connected to an intraphysical consciousness. In this case, the extraphysical consciousness can contribute with productive thoughts and energetic patterns, for example, in an interaction that promotes the growth of the intraphysical consciousness. The extraphysical consciousness that works in this manner is called a *helper* in the context of conscientiology.

In conclusion, the auric coupling can be more productive or less productive from the personal growth perspective, depending on specific traits of those involved. This is a complex subject, hard to summarize in a few paragraphs, however, this brief introduction is necessary as clairvoyance can be a tool to identifying the presence of such energy couplings.

The Vibrational State, presented later in Chapter 7, "Preparation Exercises," is a bioenergetic state that breaks the auric coupling and can be achieved through Closed Circuit of Energies, also presented in that chapter.

Perception and Manifestation

Each one of us – a consciousness – interacts with others and with the surrounding environment through perception and manifestation. Manifestation occurs when a consciousness sends out information or changes the surroundings through some action.

To speak is a manifestation, the same way as to write or to wave hello to a neighbor. To set the table for dinner is also a manifestation, since the table will look different afterward.

We can also think of manifestations beyond the physical body or the physical dimension. If I think of a friend, I will inevitably be sending my energies in his direction, that is, my manifestation is the thosene I produced.

Perception means receiving information. This can happen through bioenergies, movements that we perceive, or words we hear, for example. A perception can happen through your physical body or through the other vehicles described earlier: energosoma, psychosoma, and mentalsoma.

If I arrive at home and feel that it is very cold indoors, it means that I have the perception that the temperature is low. In this case, I perceived that the temperature was low through my soma (physical body).

Now, suppose that, when arriving at my workplace, I perceive an atmosphere of happiness and optimism before I see any of my coworkers or have any physical indication that would suggest this to me. I could have perceived this with my *energosoma*, in other words, I was able to read information from the holothosene of my workplace. In this case the information in the extraphysical energies reached me via parapsychism.

A classic example of extraphysical perception and manifestation is when we think about someone and seconds later this person call us on the phone.

This happens because while dialing the number and waiting for the connection to be established, they are normally thinking about the person who is going to get the call. This provokes a natural telepathy, or manifestation of the thought with energies. The person who gets the call, in turn, thinks of the one who made the call due to the perception of the energies carrying thoughts and feelings (thosenes) being received. In other words, the person had a thought before receiving the call due to an extraphysical perception.

The term parapsychism includes "both sides of the coin" perception and manifestation. In phenomena like intuition and psychometry, which are examples of parapsychic perception, we receive information of extraphysical origin. During an exteriorization of energies, or when ideas are sent via telepathy, the information is sent outwards, characterizing manifestation.

An aspect of extraphysical perception that is a bit more complex, particular in the beginning, when you are starting to experiment with this type of perception, is that perceptions can come from different sources and present themselves in a very similar way. An experimenter can find it hard to differentiate telepathy from intuition, for example, especially when not a lot of experiences have been accumulated, analyzed, understood, and classified.

With more training, it is possible to identify the source of the perception more easily. It helps to be attentive to minutiae, to the smallest details of the perception. You should not be discouraged if you cannot identify the source of some perceptions; this is part of multidimensional life. As you develop your parapsychism, the proportion of perceptions that make sense and that you can trace it back to the source, should increase gradually.

As for physical perception, identifying the source is something simple, natural. For instance, to see and to touch an object are experiences that are very different. Identifying and remembering if the source of a perception was hearing or vision is considered straightforward to most. It would be somewhat absurd if someone told you "I do not remember if I heard the music or only saw the musician playing it."

Clairvoyance is an extraphysical visual perception, independent from the soma. It is, therefore, independent from physical vision or physical eyes, retina, nerve tissue, and brain. Those physical components are not necessary for clairvoyance perception.

Clairvoyance allows visual perception of energies and consciousnesses (spirits) in extraphysical dimensions. We will explore the differences between clairvoyance and other forms of perception in the chapter "Clairvoyance and Other Phenomena."

Parapsychism

In the context of multiple dimensions, parapsychism means the ability to perceive dimensions other than the physical one. *Psychism* is normally understood as the ability to perceive the physical world. The prefix *para* in parapsychism indicates that it brings information from non-physical dimensions.

To see the aura through clairvoyance is a form of parapsychism. To feel that the energies of a friend are positive is parapsychism. But the cold sensation in your hand when you hold a cup of iced water is a physical perception.

The separation between the two is not always as clear-cut as in the examples above, but the intention is to give basic parameters so that the experimenter can start collecting personal references. In practice, we can feel a "touch" from an extraphysical consciousness, or something that *feels* cold but has a bioenergetic, extraphysical origin.

Differentiating what is physical from what is extraphysical requires experience, or external verification. Both can give us certainty about the origin of the perception. An iterative learning process and attention to detail is what will ultimately bring answers to the questions: did something physical touch me, or was it an extraphysical consciousness? Was this sensation of change in temperature something physical or bioenergetic?

The distinction is important since it draws a line between two major ways we can receive information: via physical body or via non-physical vehicles. When we look at a person we see their physical body via physical eyes. We can also perceive characteristics of her energies via parapsychism.

It is also important to differentiate physical from extraphysical perception to increase the objectivity of the experiences in multiple dimensions. Otherwise we would be at the risk of incorrectly interpreting a physical perception, confounding it with parapsychism or vice-versa.

For example: Fernando can say he did not like Tony's energies when, in fact, what he did not like was Tony's personality.

We have already indicated that more objective multidimensional perceptions depend on experience. Additionally, the variety and quality of those experiences, followed by analysis and reflection would help a lot. A key factor in parapsychic development is the practice of self-observation. Deeper self-knowledge will also favor the identification of the origin of our perceptions.

Another useful skill is to learn how to separate interpretation from perception. When seeing an extraphysical consciousness with a bright aura, a Buddhist may say, "I saw Buddha," whereas a Christian may say, "I saw an angel," and a third person may say, "I saw Johnny, a friend from my childhood."

The objective fact in the example above could be expressed as "I saw an extraphysical consciousness enveloped in bright light." The interpretations can be many, but it is worthwhile to write down or communicate the details of this perception separately from the interpretation. The goal is to apply a scientific approach even to subjective phenomena and give us a better chance of an objective assessment of the experience. This should hopefully allow us to take more from those experiences in the long run.

You can also write down your interpretation or hypothesis separately, allowing you to revisit the experience in the future and see if your conclusions change as you accumulate experiences.

Paraperceptiology and Projectiology

The study of clairvoyance is directly connected with a specialty of conscientiology called paraperceptiology, the study of the para-perceptions of the consciousness, beyond the perceptions of the human body (soma), and its phenomena and evolutionary consequences.

As discussed previously, clairvoyance is a *para*perception of the psychosoma, an *extra*physical body, which makes this a *para*psychic perception, beyond the physical body.

Projectiology is a specialty of conscientiology that studies the interactions of the consciousness beyond the physical body.

Although the central phenomenon of projectiology is the out-of-body experience, there are several topics that are useful and applicable to clairvoyance. For example, the study of dimensions and interactions with extraphysical dimensions is very relevant to both clairvoyance and the OBE.

Chapter 2

Perception of Images

The consciousness can have experiences that involve images in different ways. We can passively receive images when we look at a landscape or actively create a mental image of how a character looks in a book we are reading.

Additionally, the images perceived by us may originate from different sources, such as,

1. Physical Visual Perception (eyes, brain)
2. Memory (brain)
3. Holomemory (*para*brain)
4. Dream, hypnagogic state (brain)
5. Imagination, visualization (mentalsoma, brain)
6. Clairvoyance (psychosoma)

The set of sources above is a good representation of what you can expect in the clairvoyance exercises described in the subsequent chapters. There are more sources and possibilities however, for now, we will look into each of the sources listed above, in detail, and try to outline how it can be differentiated from clairvoyance.

It is also possible that the resulting image we perceive comes from more than one source. We will approach each source in isolation at first, and later explore the possible combinations.

Physical Visual Perception

This is the most common type of image perception, and probably the most studied in modern history. In essence, our eyes and brain are responsible for physical vision. Light emitted or reflected from objects in front of us reach our retina, then are transformed in electrical pulses and transmitted to the brain via optical nerve. Our brain does a great deal of processing of this input signal and we, consciousness, have access to these processed images.

Stating the obvious, I am going to say that the information that reaches our eyes is from the present. If we see Maria in front of us it is because she *is* in front of us and not because she *was* or *will be* there. This may sound a bit silly, but it will make sense later when we examine this variable in other forms of visual experience.

Beyond normal perception through our eyes, the physical body can also present images to the consciousness in events of visual hallucination. In this case, the consciousness can perceive objects, colors, people, or landscapes that, in reality, are not being captured by physical vision. The images are generated directly in the brain, in a pathological condition, or some abnormal functioning of the soma. Hallucinations can happen in cases of extreme high fever, extreme dehydration, intoxication with hallucinogenic drugs, for example.

Conventional science has accumulated a great deal of information about the retina, globe, optical nerve and regions of the brain dedicated to image processing. It is known that this physical perception is highly sophisticated, but also that it can be "fooled" or "become confused" in certain conditions, as it is the case in optical illusions.

Although clairvoyance is independent from physical vision, some preparation techniques presented in this book, work with characteristics of physical vision. Learning how to operate certain aspects of physical vision will help you train on how to operate "internal" aspects of your holosoma, aspects that cannot be demonstrated by someone else, or explained in a diagram – a key problem with subjective phenomena. We will work with a two-step sequence: (1) describe subjective experiences, (2) attempt to generate those experiences at will. This methodology applies to both physical vision and to clairvoyance, so we will start with some elements of physical vision, then work towards paravision.

Memory

Think about where you lived when you were 15 years old. Think about the main entrance door, then the bedroom where you used to sleep, the details around, and the color of the walls. As you recall such details, you have probably "seen" images of the place you used to live inside your head. As you attempt to recall the entrance door, you issued a command to retrieve the image seen and acquired in the past. The door, naturally, was not in front of you. The image you have "seen" came from your physical memory, from your brain, as it is a memory from this life.

Holomemory

We also store images, sounds, and information from past lives and from periods between lives (intermissive periods). If the information comes from before we were born, and even before we were conceived in this life, then it is not possible that they are stored in your physical brain, as this physical structure did not exist before you were born.

The memory that includes this life *and* past lives receives the name of *holo*memory. The consciousness can, in certain conditions, retrieve information from areas of the holomemory that belong to periods before this current physical life. Past life recalls are often visual experiences, and the scenes and information accessed comes from the holomemory of the experimenter.

Oneiric Images

Dreaming is an altered state of consciousness that also brings images to the consciousness. A widely accepted theory in conventional science is that oneiric images, the images you see in the dreaming state, are related to emotions and events we experience in the waking state.

The logic and events in a dream are normally different from what we would expect in the waking state. A lot of the dreams are symbolic and do not mean literally what is being portrayed, and lots of dreams may appear nonsensical and disconnected from our reality.

There is another altered state of consciousness where oneiric images are often experienced, the hypnagogic state. When you are at the edge between the waking state and the sleep state, close to letting go of all controls of your thought processes, but still lucid enough to capture the experience, you may start to see images and sometimes hear sounds in your "mental screen."

Generally speaking, the source of images in the hypnagogic state is the same as in a dream: your physical brain. As we relax and our body goes towards the sleep state, a few changes happen in our physiology: the temperature of our body can decrease slightly, muscles relax, and your heatbeat rate slows down. One of the interesting changes in this process is when a certain function ceases to be controlled by our will power and becomes controlled by our soma, by the part of the brain dedicated to "automatic" processes.

Breathing is a good example of this transition: as we fall asleep, our physical body controls breathing automatically. Similarly, as we fall asleep, our brain begins to operate farther from the control of our will. When we are awake we have a higher control of our thoughts. Not full control, of course, at least not all the time. Try to think about a single subject without dispersing, or daydreaming, for ten minutes and you will understand the problem.

Our physical brain is constantly connecting ideas and, usually, after few minutes we will be thinking about a subject that is far from the original topic proposed.

There are several theories to explain dreams. One of the most accepted theories from conventional science is, in a simplified explanation, that dreams are a byproduct of reorganization processes related to synapses, the connections between neurons, and general biochemical "cleansing" of the brain. Images are generated while we sleep and the brain is preparing "the machinery" for the next day.

It is not difficult to differentiate dreams from clairvoyance. The sequence of ideas, shapes, and how we move from one place to the next, for example, follow a peculiar logic. We tend not to question this logic when we are dreaming, even when it is absurd. The contrast with the real world becomes evident after we wake up and recall the dream.

For instance, suppose that while reading this book at home your doorbell rings. And suppose that, as you open the door, you see two zebras smiling at you. The zebras then introduce themselves as your new neighbors, telling you they just moved in. What would your reaction be?

I would bet you would be, at the very least, surprised and intrigued. Where did those talking zebras come from? Did they run away from the zoo? Am I okay? Is this a hallucination or the effect of some medicine or spoiled food that I ingested? The absurdity of the situation would be clear with waking state reasoning. In a dream, the absurdity would only become evident after you wake up and recall the dream. In dreaming, our reactions to absurd situations can also be absurd: we could invite the zebras to come in for a coffee. This is due to the characteristic of low lucidity of the consciousness (us) during the experience.

As for the hypnagogic state, the differentiation usually requires a bit more training and observation. If you close your eyes and try to relax before going to sleep you will, at some point, go through the hypnagogic state. If you go to sleep very quickly it may be so fast that you will not notice it.

An account from a student of one of the courses, while trying an exercise with bioenergies:

[...] at some point during the exercise I started to see colors and

geometric shapes in front of me. I could see those images floating in the space, sometimes with more brightness, sometimes with less. I also heard a nice gentle music, hard to describe. The images were changing and I was entertained. Some faces appeared... After that, a street in a city I do not recall ever visiting. Then I heard the instructor voice "stay lucid." The images disappeared and I reconnected with my surroundings.

What happened was that the student was relaxed but allowed her lucidity to drop to a lower level and entered the hypnagogic state. At the end, the instructor voice – a physical stimuli – brought her back and increased her lucidity. The account is a good illustration of how a lower lucidity is equivalent to "holding the reins a bit more loosely," or to allow the brain to work a bit more independently and in its own internal processes, generating the images described by the student.

The key difference between clairvoyance and the hypnagogic state is the source of the images. Oneiric images from the hypnagogic state come from the brain and are not the result of a perception. Clairvoyance, in turn, is a perception of the psychosoma, of something beyond the physical dimension and external to the consciousness.

Now, clairvoyance is independent from physical vision and, technically, we could do it with our eyes closed. The problem is that within minutes in this condition most people end up in the hypnagogic state at some point. At the end, it could be hard to differentiate what was clairvoyance from what was hypnagogic state, especially for those with less overall parapsychic experience.

It is also possible that paravision is combined with oneiric images. For example, you could see the face of an extraphysical consciousness very close to your own face, perhaps around five inches away (clairvoyance) and, in the background, you see dunes in a desert landscape (oneiric image). A lower lucidity during the experience makes it harder to identify the source of the images.

All that complexity goes away if you apply clairvoyance techniques with your eyes open. Entering the hypnagogic state with your eyes open would be very difficult. This would help you eliminate several hypotheses, because what you will see – with physical vision or paravision – comes from an external source, not from your brain.

This is the main reason why we suggest that you apply techniques with your eyes open: to eliminate one possible source of images, those from the hypnagogic state.

Imagination, Visualization

To visualize or to imagine is as different from clairvoyance as it is from seeing something with your physical eyes. To imagine means to create an image by acting with your physical brain and mentalsoma.

You can imagine the paper on the pages of this book are green, even with your eyes open. If you are lucid, however, and compare the color green with the actual color of the paper, you will quickly see that the pages are not printed (or displayed) in green paper. The lucidity aspect here is important: being in a lucid state helps with this assessment.

There are authors that differentiate imagining from visualizing, stating that imagination is inside one's head and visualization is in a specific place in space, which can be outside one's head. For example, I can look at my right hand and visualize a peach in my hand. The fact that the peach is in that specific place, and not in my "mental screen," would mean that this is a visualization.

On a contrasting example, I can close my eyes and imagine that I am in front of a tranquil lake, and imagine the water and scenery around me, the sky and the clouds. In this case, the landscape is created "inside" my head, which would classify the experience as imagination.

The term imagination is also used for things that are more abstract and not necessarily have a defined shape or form. For example, one could say, "imagine the perfume of a bouquet of flowers."

A key element for both visualization and imagination is the presence of a willful action *during* the experience. For a healthy person in the normal waking state, the passive observation focused on external stimuli excludes imagination and visualization. In other words, it is necessary to *want* to imagine, to give a mental command. The same applies to visualization. The origin of the images that we imagine or visualize is the consciousness herself: she generates a visual experience using her mentalsoma.

Imagination and visualization have no room to exist if you remove the will power, or the *"I want to visualize"* and put yourself in a passive and receptive condition.

Another aspect is that even if we apply a lot of effort in the visualization, the level of clarity of the images is never as good as in a clairvoyance or physical vision experience. In the example of visualizing a peach in your hand, you *know* that the peach is not there.

Therefore, if we remove the effort to imagine during our observation there is no way to confuse imagination with clairvoyance, especially when you have your eyes open and your soma is operating in normal healthy conditions. If you, in those conditions, see a bright three-inch contour around the person you are looking at when applying a technique, then this is clairvoyance.

Clairvoyance

This is the extraphysical mode of visual perception. As presented earlier, this type of perception is independent from your soma, brain and physical eyes.

Clairvoyance is also independent from physical forces such as electrical fields, magnetic fields, gravitational fields, and other known physical forces present in nature.

This independence from the physical body can be verified through personal experience: you can observe the aura of a person during an out-of-body experience. Moreover, you can find a consciousness in the extraphysical dimension that already died, and therefore has no physical body, and verify that the extraphysical consciousness can still see auras, energies, and the psychosoma of other consciousnesses – including yours – while projected.

Clairvoyance can be experienced in complete absence of any source of visible light. It can be started and stopped directly at will, dispensing even techniques and procedures.

There is no need for equipment, incense, crystals, amulets, or any physical material. The simple act of looking for this type of perception and being more open to it can be enough to trigger paravision.

Prayer, mantras or rituals are also not necessary for the extraphysical vision. And, considering the long term benefits we are seeking, those practices are not desired nor indicated, despite its occasional efficacy, as those do not help to increase self-confidence, self-reliance, and tend to perpetuate a cycle of restrictive indoctrination that prevents achieving a higher lucidity.

Model of Multidimensional Visual Perception

An analogy that I use to explain how physical and extraphysical visual perception are combined is composed of two screens.

In the picture opposite, the screen that is the farthest from the observer is opaque, like a screen we would find in a movie theatre. The screen closer to the observer, the first screen, is semitransparent. The observer can see things in this first screen but also see through it, so the second screen on the background is also visible.

In this analogy, the images in the second screen, the farthest

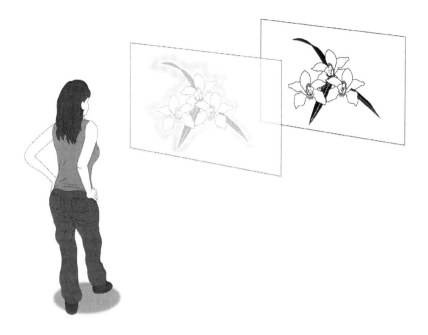

Figure 1: Model of Multidimensional Visual Perception

one, represent the physical vision. The images in the first screen, the semitransparent and closer one, represent clairvoyance.

What we see through our physical vision is clear and objective to us. In the screens analogy, this is equivalent to saying that the second screen is so bright that it makes it hard to perceive the faint images on the first screen.

We also instinctively make an effort to stay tuned to the physical vision. If we see something that is not considered normal, or something we do not expect, we may blink, rub our eyes, move our head, adjust our glasses, if we are wearing any. We take a second look. In the analogy, all those actions are equivalent to making the physical screen even brighter, which would make it harder to see any extraphysical image on the first screen.

A friend of mine described one of his clairvoyance experiences where he was watching TV very late at night. Everything was very silent at that time of night, and at some point he saw someone walking in the hallway about five yards to his left. He saw this person at "the corner of his eye," or in the periphery of his vision, and his natural reaction was to turn his head towards the hallway – where he saw someone – and verify if she was still there. He did not expect anyone there: no one else was at home at that time.

Moving your head quickly can be a problem when you are applying a clairvoyance technique, as this would make the clairvoyance perceptions less visible. And this was exactly what happened with my friend: he "switched off" clairvoyance as he moved his head, and was unable to verify the presence of the consciousness he has seen earlier. The slight disconnection of the psychosoma that probably triggered clairvoyance was gone with the quick movement.

We can, of course, learn to trigger and keep our clairvoyance "on" in the waking state, even while moving our physical body. The approach used in this book, however, is very much focused in being still and deepening the relaxation, which provides better conditions to learn how to operate the "switch" that turns clairvoyance on and to keep it going for longer periods. With time, you will develop the ability to access your clairvoyance in a wider variety of conditions.

In the analogy of screens, we will be trying to reduce the brightness of the physical vision so that images in the clairvoyance screen are more easily detected. We will do this through relaxation, by avoiding physical movement, especially avoiding moving our head and eyes, and dimming the lights.

Chapter 3

Why Develop Clairvoyance?

Some of the reasons presented in this chapter may include the reason you became interested in clairvoyance. Many start studying themes such as this one due to curiosity mixed with a feeling that there is more to life than the physical dimension.

For one reason or another, we tend to focus most of our time and energy in physical things, or more immediate needs. Taking time to study, reflect, and go deeper in researching what is "out there" tends to be an exception. A few would dedicate larger amounts of time on the question "what are we doing here?"

Perhaps the most important reason to develop clairvoyance – and psychic ability in general – is to work with this and many other existential questions. The development of parapsychism represents a new form of perception of the reality surrounding us, and tremendously expands the possibilities in this search.

Multidimensional Self-Awareness

Clairvoyance increases our knowledge and practical experience of what happens around us and in multiple dimensions.

The word "clairvoyance" originated in medieval French: *Clervoyance* (1580, *clair* of clear, *voyence* for capacity to see).

If, on the one hand, the original meaning of the word clairvoyance may come across as a bit presumptuous, since those who see "only" the physical dimension seem to be in disadvantage, on the other, it highlights the notion that a purely physical perception offers a limited picture of reality.

It is relatively easy to *believe* in clairvoyance. To read or listen to third-party accounts can help in understanding the phenomenon and to widen the knowledge of this subject. However, it is important to keep in perspective that *personal experience* is what will help you realize long-term benefits connected to personal growth.

Multidimensional Self-Awareness (MSA) means to be aware of multiple dimensions, including non-physical ones, through personal experience. It means validating theory through parapsychic practice, to be able to describe experiences you had yourself, in detail.

And why is multidimensional self-awareness important? Because it represents the tip of an extremely interesting iceberg, one that offers new possibilities and new ways of interpreting what happens to you, with basis on a new paradigm where you are consciousness in evolution. In this paradigm, you are a consciousness that had multiple lives and will have many others that interacts with consciousnesses in this and other dimensions, with cause and effect logic that goes beyond the physical world, and beyond the consensus understanding and conventions from society.

The experience with this new paradigm can help to explore questions such as is there a life mission or life task? Is there life after death? If there is, what are the implications? Is the concept of cause and effect extensible to energies and interactions with others across multiple lives? Do we have a duty to help others? And what is the effect of helping in my evolution? Why do I see myself in situations I don't like, is it karma? How much importance should I give to my time? Am I giving priority to what is really important for my evolution? Am I behaving with sufficient maturity, as a consciousness, in the roles I play in life?

Developing your psychic ability without mysticism or indoctrination is one of the factors that contribute to an expanded multidimensional self-awareness. Incorporating extraphysical elements to our understanding of how things work can promote change in our values and priorities, and offer a more complete picture of what is happening around us in our day-to-day life.

Multidimensional self-awareness will also expand the understanding of life's events in general and can deepen the knowledge we have about ourselves.

Fast and Easy Development

Because clairvoyance does not need a deeper altered state of consciousness induced by deeper levels of relaxation, it is more accessible even to people that never practiced similar techniques.

Additionally, the majority of techniques can be applied with your eyes open, which helps to maintain the lucidity and avoiding entering the sleep state, daydreaming, or the hypnagogic state.

From the experience gathered in clairvoyance workshops I have seen that with about three hours of theory followed by another three hours of practice, the vast majority of people reported clairvoyance perceptions.

Although there are forms of clairvoyance that may take years to develop, such as seeing extraphysical consciousnesses directly and in daylight, you will be able to gauge your progress clearly as you apply techniques.

For example, you can see the denser parts of the energy dimension with only a few hours of effort, while it may take a few days to develop the perception of specific chakras. With a few weeks of practice, you would be able to see the first layer of the aura. Later, maybe with practice measured in months, you start seeing the outer layer of the aura, and so on. The constant progress will keep you motivated to learn, in practice, the fascinating aspects of this form of parapsychism.

Other Parapsychic Abilities

Extraphysical vision help to promoted the development of other parapsychic abilities. Among the many ways you can have contact with non-physical dimensions, the out-of-body experience (OBE, astral projection) is probably the most impactful and productive in terms of personal growth.

In order to achieve a lucid OBE, however, you need to let your physical body go to sleep and somehow stay lucid. Your soma will be sleeping while you, consciousness, will stay awake. For this reason, it would be impractical, for example, to have an OBE at your workplace in a normal working day, you would have to wait for a quiet evening or weekend to apply your techniques.

Although the effects of the OBE – like changes in principles and values – would stay with you 24 hours a day, the OBE itself is not an experience for your day-to-day waking state.

There are accounts of OBEs with the physical body in movement, but those experiences tend to be rare and of very short duration.

Paravision, by contrast, is something that can work in your waking state life and contribute to make your routine less restricted to the physical dimension, which will help to increase your multidimensional self-awareness.

The distance between the physical dimension and the extra-physical dimensions is shortened when clairvoyance is included in the list of possible daily perceptions. As a consequence, an experimenter that has paravision experiences would be, in practice, less materialistic, and more sensitive and lucid to the multidimensional reality.

Self-Confidence and Parapsychism

A motivating factor of paravision is that it is a phenomenon that people do not feel afraid of, generally speaking, even for those without prior parapsychic experiences. Some clairvoyance techniques can work with a relatively "shallow" level of relax-ation, where the person feels in control of the process, and with open eyes and even in a well-lit room.

I must say that the fear of any type of parapsychism is not necessary, as those are natural abilities. The extraphysical realities will not change with us being able to see them or not.

Fearing psychic experiences can have many sources. Movies,

books, and documentaries often approach the phenomena from a sensationalist perspective. Horror and suspense films make matters worse and often give emphasis in negative aspects, portraying those with psychic abilities as abnormalities.

A brain tumor, brain damage, lightning strike, or exposure to specific substances is often portrayed as the cause of the parapsychic ability in a movie character. In real life, however, I have never seen this correlation and, instead, have seen hundreds of physically and mentally healthy people describing logical, coherent parapsychic perceptions.

Some religions may also instill fear, directly or indirectly through dogmatic teachings, at times, perhaps, with the intention to keep the followers dependent, or to avoid that specific dogmas are seen as incoherent. Constructive extra-physical experiences could also break the continuity of certain traditions and rituals, as they could be seen as illogical when a wider group comes into more direct contact with extraphysical realities.

There are also the remnants of the secret society culture from the Middle Ages, where mystery and unnecessary complexity end up producing a certain suspicion and lack of understanding which, ultimately, lead to fear.

One of the ways to gain confidence in your own parapsychic capacity is the prophylactic riddance of all of all types of mysticism, adopting a positive and pragmatic posture towards multidimensionality. If the intention is to learn and to help, the pattern of energies (holothosene) will be positive and, as a consequence, an atmosphere favorable to experiences that promote personal growth will be created, with nothing to fear.

Another way is to start with the basic exercises with bioenergy, in order to feel that the process is under control, developing confidence through repetition. After that, you can work your way through preparation exercises, and build your confidence further as you go along.

If an experimenter completes ten exercises where he was able to perceive the energies or to see the energosoma of someone else, then parapsychism will feel more accessible, controllable. Afterwards, the same experimenter will be more inclined to try deeper levels of relaxation in order to access other types of experience. Applying techniques in lower lighting conditions will also feel less intimidating, as the whole process is de-dramatized.

In summary, clairvoyance can be used as an entry point to other types of parapsychism. This is equivalent to getting into the water slowly, progressively, starting on the shallow side of the pool, then learning how to swim before venturing into deeper areas.

Feel at Ease with Extraphysical People

After some years of workshops for parapsychic development, a few patterns of participant behavior and personality profiles become evident. One of the patterns is the individual that has a good amount of technical information about the extraphysical dimensions, a few practical experiences, and a lot of fear of extraphysical consciousnesses.

A person with this profile would freeze if an extraphysical consciousness became visible in his bedroom, even without information about the intention and quality of energies of this consciousness – good, bad, or neutral. Seeing an extraphysical consciousness provokes panic.

Such reaction indicates lack of parapsychic maturity from the experimenter. A low number of experiences or lack of "processing" experiences in a healthy, productive way, is the main factor here. Parapsychic maturity would bring a calm response and perhaps a bit of curiosity, a spirit of investigation about the extraphysical consciousness detected at any given moment.

Quantity of experiences alone is not the solution, since staying confident during a parapsychic experience depends on the experimenter's personality, the nature of the experience, and the understanding we have of that experience as it is happening.

Parapsychic experimentation of multidimensionality, when done in a controlled way, can help to build confidence and maturity. Working with energies and creating your own field – through the exteriorization technique we will discuss later on – and maintaining a positive pattern of thoughts and sentiments will set the stage for a parapsychic experience that contributes to increased consciential maturity.

A person that has seen "ghosts" several times in such controlled conditions would have this positive "boldness" towards this type of paravision.

Since clairvoyance is a phenomenon relatively accessible and controllable, such experiences work as a step towards gaining more confidence to develop other forms of parapsychic ability.

Lucidity and Visual Perception

In the Chapter 2, topic "Perception of Images" we explored several ways in which we can have visual experiences, including physical vision and clairvoyance.

Several of the techniques presented later in this book, work with improving acuity of physical perception as a step in clairvoyance development. Developing visual acuity and practicing how to describe what you see in deeper detail is also useful for us to be more "present" in our day to day life. Paying closer attention to your visual perception can make you more aware of what is happening around you, it can make you more lucid, more receptive.

As I started to study clairvoyance more deeply, I felt the need to learn more about my own visual perception. In this process I started to perceive nuances of reflections, textures, hues, various levels of luminosity, and different types of finishes in objects that I had never before realized.

Extraphysical Beings

Jane, one of the participants of a workshop, reported that, as she visited an apartment while searching for a new place to live, she felt a strange "atmosphere" right after going through the door. Something in that environment produced an unpleasant sensation. Jane attributed this sensation to the presence of extraphysical consciousnesses that were creating that pattern of energies (holothosene).

In a case like this one, clairvoyance could be used to identify the presence of "spirits" (extraphysical consciousnesses, conscexes), and confirm the first parapsychic reading.

Visually detecting an extraphysical consciousness usually happens in an indirect way: you do not necessarily see the extraphysical consciousness per se, face, clothes and all detail. You see, instead, the effects of the energy around the extraphysical consciousness, typically the contour or envelope of energies around her, or a flash, or bright spots moving around a specific area.

Parapsychic perceptions could then help to assess if the house you are planning to buy, or to rent, already has extraphysical residents.

When my wife and I started the refurbishment of an apartment that we had recently acquired, we felt the presence of an extraphysical consciousness. The sensation was stronger when we started to rip the wallpaper in the kitchen.

As I had perceived this presence a few times on that day, I mentioned this fact to Patricia, who then told me that she also perceived an extraphysical consciousness in several moments.

The extraphysical consciousness was not negative, but made it clear through her thosenes that she was not happy with the changes in the apartment. We did notice, before buying the fully furnished property that the decoration was very particular, suggesting a careful selection of each element of the overall design. We bought the apartment from the heirs of a lady that used to live there and died in a nearby hospital a few months earlier.

As we interacted with the consciousness and with a bit of common sense, we connected the dots: The extraphysical consciousness was the former owner of the apartment. One out-of-body experience and a few clairvoyance observations gave support to the hypothesis.

With that knowledge, we "extended" the renovation to the extraphysical dimension. We worked with energy, mainly exteriorizing (see preparation exercises), with a diplomatic and assertive pattern of thought, along the lines of

Listen, I know you like this place very much and how it was decorated, but we now live here and you no longer need a house, as you are now an extraphysical consciousness, you can be free from the physical world and explore your new condition. We will make several modifications and will imprint our own pattern of energies here...

With time, the extraphysical consciousness probably understood her new situation and reduced her attachment to that physical place. We stopped feeling her presence about two weeks after we finished the renovation.

Energetic Coupling

As presented in Chapter 1, the energetic coupling is based on some point of affinity among the consciousnesses involved: a thought pattern, activity, or emotion, for instance.

When two consciousnesses are connected energetically in this fashion the shape of the aura can change. This is true for any combination of intraphysical and extraphysical participants. You can detect this change of shape via clairvoyance, meaning, you can visually detect when two or more consciousnesses are energetically coupled.

If you meet a friend with whom you have a lot of affinity, it would be natural to engage in an auric coupling after a few minutes of conversation. If a third person looks at the two of you from a few yards away, you would see something more or less like this:

Figure 2: Auric Coupling

If the auric coupling happens between an intraphysical consciousness and an extraphysical consciousness, we would be able to see changes in the external region of the psychosphere, in shapes similar to this:

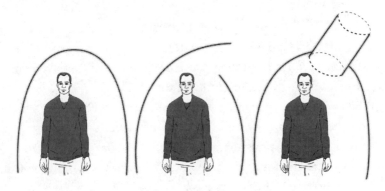

Figure 3: Changes in the External Region of the Aura

The perception of changes in the shape of someone's aura does not necessarily offer information about the quality of the extraphysical consciousness connected to that person. In order to identify the quality of the extraphysical consciousness you need to perform an energetic reading of her.

Still, the simple fact of identifying that someone has or not an energetically connected extraphysical companion is a piece of information that can help us understand the multidimensional context of the conversation.

For example, if you detect that Maria is energetically coupled with an extraphysical consciousness you can start to ask – why this companion? And since energetic coupling is based on affinity, mainly on holothosene affinity, you can also ask – which pattern of ideas and sentiments is Maria expressing at that moment? You can also ask – is this the baseline pattern of Maria, or is the presence of the conscex changing her behavior? In what way? Is she more lucid or less lucid at this moment? More pacifying or more conflictive?

To perceive extraphysical presences through clairvoyance leads to a series of possible connections, both in physical and extraphysical terms.

And this is exactly what enhances your multidimensional experience. An ordinary conversation, which would normally be forgotten in minutes, can become a rich and interesting interaction that contributes to your personal evolution, parapsychic maturity, and ability to help.

Confirming Perceptions

Paravision can be used to confirm other forms of extraphysical perception. Imagine the following scenario: you work in a place where one of your colleagues displays unusual variations in his mood over the week. One day he is perfectly fine and, on the next, he is excessively cynical and aggressive, with no apparent logic or reason.

Cases like this can be explained by the presence of extra-physical companions that influence this coworker. In the "good" days, there is no connection or presence of negative extraphysical companions. On the "bad" days, one or more extraphysical consciousnesses are energetically connected to your colleague, in a way that promotes and amplifies negative aggressiveness.

Now suppose that you need to discuss complex work issues that include criticism to some decisions made by this colleague. It would be smart to pick a "good" day for this. And, of course, detecting the presence of extraphysical presences could help. There are a few ways to accomplish this, with several modes of parapsychic ability, for example, intuition, energy reading, and clairvoyance.

If you develop more than one mode of perception you will be able to gather stronger evidence from extraphysical dimensions. Intuition could be a good source; however, since this perception arrives with no explanation, context, or reasoning, it is hard to trust it. If you had the intuition and later detected that the shape of the aura of your colleague has changed, then the combination of both perceptions would give you stronger support to the hypothesis.

And extraphysical presences are often perceived by intuition or quick energetic perceptions. In this context, clairvoyance can be a great instrument to validate further such perceptions.

This is not to say that any particular mode of parapsychic perception is superior from another. The point is that looking for confirmation and at the interplay of several modes of parapsychism is a great approach to getting more information from any multidimensional event.

Having said that, we also have to keep in mind that some types of information are more easily detected with specific parapsychic abilities. Auric couplings are more easily detected through clairvoyance, and quality of energies is more easily detected via psychometry.

Chapter 4

Paravision Characteristics

Can be Learned and Developed

Clairvoyance is a consciential ability that can be developed by anyone, including those without prior parapsychic experience. All that is needed is a bit of technique and dedication.

As it is the case of any human ability, we will find people with a lot of talent with this particular trait and that can trigger clairvoyance with very little effort. We will also find people that develop it naturally in their childhood. Some are able to describe visual perceptions from other dimensions in their very first attempt. For most, however, a bit of time and persistence are required to reach a good level of clairvoyance.

So it is expected that in a group of 20 people, for instance, the speed of development will not be uniform. Every individual has a specific set of abilities that has been developed in this and other lives, in specific circumstances and specific experiences.

Generally speaking, those who have a better ability to relax and concentrate will find it easier to develop the extraphysical vision. Chapter 7, "Preparation Exercises," presents several basic abilities, including those two that facilitate parapsychic development.

In my case, the development of clairvoyance was from "absolute zero." In the first exercises I could not see anything beyond the physical dimension, no matter how much effort I applied. I recall classes that I participated, in Curitiba, Brazil, where everyone but me reported interesting perceptions. I could not see anything extraphysical. I do not consider myself special or someone with an exceptional paravision ability today. However, considering that I started with nothing, and that I reached the level of perception and control of the phenomenon that I have today, I can say that the progress is visible – literally.

Capacity to Magnify (Zoom)

Something interesting in clairvoyance is the possibility to magnify, apparently without limits, the size of the object under observation. Some accounts describe perception of detail of very small objects or insects measured in a few millimeters, even when seen from a distance, as if those where tens or hundreds of times bigger. Waldemar von Wasielewski (1875 – 1959) is one of the authors that collected accounts of this kind of perception.

Though the mechanism of this type of perception is not known at the moment, those accounts indicate that the perception is independent from several aspects of physical optics.

It Is Independent from Physical Eyes

In an out-of-body experience, the capacity to see is clearly not dependent on the physical eyes – and not dependent on the physical body for that matter. When out of the body, seeing is not even restricted to your para-eyes or para-head. It is as if the entire surface of the psychosoma can receive visual images. If you place your hand behind an object that would block your vision, if it came from your paraeyes, you would be able to see behind that object, as you would be able to see with your parahand.

An interesting question derived from this characteristic is – can a blind person have visual perceptions through clairvoyance or during an out-of-body experience?

This is a complex question. The theoretical and simplistic answer is yes, although in practice such cases are very rare.

Factors that contribute to the complexity of the issue are the paradigms and conditionings and how they limit our perception. This is something that applies to everyone, with functioning physical vision or not. For example, anyone can, in theory, see with 360 degrees of field of vision during an out of body experience, meaning you can see in all directions. So why is it that 360 vision is rarely reported? One hypothesis is, because we are conditioned by the experience of seeing 180 degrees (or less) during our waking state, we tend to repeat the experience and unconsciously limit our vision while out of the body.

In the case of the intraphysical consciousness that is blind, his everyday experience does not include images. The perceptive paradigm would have to be broken so he could get to visual experiences based on paravision. This is usually not trivial. To explain a visual experience to a person that has never had visual experiences is equivalent to explaining the flavor of a fruit to someone that never tasted it, and without using references to taste-related sensations.

The independence of physical and extraphysical vision stands, however. So does the possibility of overcoming our conditionings, as is the case in reports of out-of-body experiences (OBEs) and near-death experiences (NDEs) made by physically blind people that had visual experiences while out of the body. The book *Mindsight: Near-Death and Out-of-Body Experiences in the Blind*, by Kenneth Ring and Sharon Cooper, shows very interesting case studies in this field.

It Does Not Require Physical Lighting

An extraphysical body, the psychosoma, is the vehicle of our extraphysical visual perceptions. Physical light belongs to the physical dimension. The physical stimulus, light, cannot produce a non-physical perception, clairvoyance. Our physical eyes respond to physical visible light, our paravision does not.

It is then possible to see through paravision in dark environments, where there is no source of physical light. We can also have paravision perceptions in the penumbra and even in bright, well-lit environments.

An environment with reduced physical light, however, can make it easier for you to trigger clairvoyance. This seems to contradict the independence we just stated, but that is not the case. As presented in the model for visual multidimensional perception, in Chapter 2, less physical light with help to make the physical "screen" less bright. So, less light is about making it easier to detect the *para*stimulus and see what is happening in the extraphysical "screen."

One of the procedures proposed in Chapter 8, "Clairvoyance Techniques" is to attempt to trigger your paravision during sunrise and sunset, with the objective of reducing the physical stimulus and facilitate the detection of extraphysical vision. Another technique presented involves exercises with complete absence of physical light. Those exercises can help you validate that clairvoyance is independent from physical light.

The majority of clairvoyance accounts I have heard happened at night or in low-light conditions. I have also heard a few cases of people that were able to see auras and extraphysical consciousnesses under direct sunlight. More common paravision perceptions under direct sunlight seems to be related to aeroenergy and fitoenergy, and we will see techniques for both in Chapter 8.

It Is Not Restricted to Space

Remote viewing, or travelling clairvoyance, allows the observation of events from thousands of miles away. A striking example is the observation of Jupiter and Jupiter's moons in 1973, by Ingo Swan, before the first probe reached that planet in 1979. Swan stated that Jupiter had planetary rings, something not confirmed and controversial at the time, and later confirmed when the Voyager probe passed by Jupiter in 1979.

Dimensional Tuning

We can tune into and filter out specific dimensions with clairvoyance, a characteristic that is absent from physical vision. In the physical dimension, if there is a chair in front of us, in a well-lit room, and if we look at it, there is no way *not* to see it. In normal environmental, somatic, and physical conditions, to look towards something is to see it.

With extraphysical vision the process is different. There are group exercises where two people looking at third one at the same time have very different perceptions. For example, one experimenter could see the coronochakra of the person in front of the room, and describe it as a luminous disc placed a few inches behind the head of that person. A second experimenter could, at the same time, see an extraphysical consciousness next

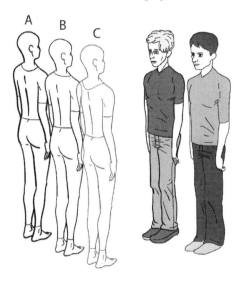

Figure 4: Three Extraphysical Consciousnesses, Two Experimenters

to the person in front of the room, while seeing no sign of the coronochakra.

The explanation is that the first experimenter was tuned into the energetic dimension, while the second was tuned into the extraphysical dimension. Both perceptions are accurate, as both the coronochakra and the extraphysical consciousness were there. However, each experimenter was able to see a *partial picture* of the reality in front of them, each one tuned into a specific dimension.

A second example of tuning involves three conscexes and two conscin-experimenters, as depicted above. The first experimenter sees conscex A only, while the second one sees A, B, and C. Something like this could happen if A was in a more dense extraphysical dimension, while B and C were in a more subtle one.

The second experimenter was able to tune a more subtle dimension than the first one. As a general rule, we can always see the dimensions that are more dense than the most subtle dimension we can reach; this is why he was able to see B, C (more subtle) *and* A (more dense).

For the first experimenter, tuned into the more dense dimension, B and C will be invisible.

Adjusting Clairvoyance Tuning to See an Aura

There are many extraphysical colors, shapes, and movements that can be identified around a person. The capacity of the experimenter to control the tuning of her clairvoyance is the main factor in determining what will be observed.

One of the most frequent perceptions, especially in the beginning of paravision development, is the energosoma around someone else. Descriptions of this perception often include the terms "bright contour," "milky white," or "white with a bit of silver," As for thickness, most report between half an inch and a couple of inches, with an average around an inch.

The energosoma can be seen around the whole body of the person, only one side, or only around the upper part of the head, or around head and shoulders.

The coronochakra is in the top rear quarter of the head, the crown area, and is normally seen as a mini-aura in the shape of a disc, around an inch from the scalp. At times it resembles a globe partially fused

Figure 5:
Energosoma

with the top of the head.

Curiously, the coronochakra is sometimes accurately pictured in some older religious paintings, where sacred beings present a disc (instead of a ring) above their head, representing the halo.

Figure 6: Coronochacra

Our aura is a type of field, resembling a bubble that envelopes our physical body and that has a typical size between 20 and 40 inches. In some cases, and in specific conditions, the aura can reach several yards.

There are two basic areas that you can identify in the aura: the internal and the external. The internal layer starts close to the skin, at the end of the energosoma, and goes up to approximately four inches. The external one starts at that point and goes up to the end of the aura.

The internal layer is more stable and this is where colors are more frequently observed. Colors often show in gradient (as opposed to solid colors). At times, it is as if this layer is "empty" or completely transparent.

The outer layer tends to be very dynamic, with constant movement. At times, the perception of this layer is fleeting, and it appears to change with every thought from the person observed. Some report seeing a series of sequential "photographs," or short periods of seeing the outer layer, followed by short periods where it disappears.

Figure 7: Inner and Outer Aura

Techniques to Change Clairvoyance Tuning

So how can you change the tuning? Considering that the command to instruct this action is subjective and internal, it is necessary to use techniques that will make the tuning change, even if indirectly, so that ultimately we learn how to control it at will.

Shifting your attention to the peripheral area of your physical vision is one of these techniques. The aim is to try to change the tuning from element of the aura to the next with this change of focal point of observation.

For example, if seeing the energosoma comes easily to you, you can keep the central point of your vision in a spot on the energosma that you can see clearly. Next, you shift your *attention*, without moving your head or your eyes, to a peripheral area of your vision, and try to see a different element of the aura. If you are looking at the energosoma on the right arm of the person, try to identify the coronochakra of this person in your peripheral vision with this technique.

As the coronochakra becomes visible, this means you have adjusted the tuning to the coronochakra "frequency." When the coronochakra is clearly visible, you can slowly move your head or eyes to put the coronochakra in the central portion of your vision, then repeat the cycle. At this point you can try to see the outer area of the aura in your peripheral vision, while having your clairvoyance "locked in" the coronochakra perception.

Another technique to learn to control the change of paravision tuning is to place the attention in a specific chakra while seeing something through clairvoyance. You may need several attempts for this to work well. Do not give up if your clairvoyance is actually switched off momentarily in the first few attempts.

The most popular chakra for this technique is the frontochakra, but you can try different ones, like the chakra in your throat (laryngochakra) or the coronochakra. You will have to split your attention in this technique, applying some of it to what you are observing, and some of it to the chakra you are trying to work on.

You need to keep about 90 percent of your attention on what you are observing through clairvoyance and about 10 percent of your attention on the chakra. This is why I refer to this procedure as the 90/10 technique.

A second technique you can use is to exteriorize energies in a very gentle way through this chakra. Shifting some of your attention to do this and the exteriorization itself can help you to "change channels" during extraphysical observation.

A third technique to change the tuning is to connect the frontochakra energetically with what you are observing by slowly exteriorizing energies toward the observation point until your energies touch it. In this case, it is common to observe a change of colors, vision of the energosoma, between your hands, and the perception of your own psychosphere from inside out.

These techniques to change the tuning work well in combination with the "Palm Chakra Field Technique" described in Chapter 8, "Clairvoyance Techniques," particularly when the chakra you choose is the frontochakra.

Positional Tuning

The second form of clairvoyance tuning has to do with position in space. This is a characteristic that does not exist in physical vision. Positional tuning allows us to see portions of physical and extraphysical dimensions as if we were slicing them, vertically, horizontally, or in any direction, in order to see a particular segment of it.

For example, let's say that we are seeing the bright contour around a person's head, which is the lateral area of energosoma, and at the same time, seeing that person's physical face clearly. With a change of positional tuning, I could see the energosoma in front of his face, perceived as a cloud or bright fog. The *dimensional* tuning remained the same: I am seeing the energetic dimension, where his energosma is. However, the *positional* tuning has changed. Instead of seeing the sides of his energosoma, I am now seeing its frontal part.

An interesting effect of positional tuning is seeing the inner side of the aura of the person observed, right behind them. This usually appears like a white translucent curtain they have leaned back upon. This perception is often combined with seeing brightness behind the person's neck, which is the nuchalchakra. Sometimes the observation of the nuchalchakra can lead to the perception of this "back curtain" perception.

A logical argument that supports the hypothesis of positional tuning is as follows: we can see the aura of others as well as our own aura. If we would always see the energies in front of us every time clairvoyance was "switched on," we would only see our own aura before any other, as it is always closer to us than any other external element. So, in order to see something that is three feet away, you would necessarily have to look "through" your own aura.

Positional tuning can help us to explore auras in more detail and see, for example, the outer skin of the first layer of the aura. This observation can happen when looking at our own aura, from inside out, or while observing another person.

Overlapping Dimensions

According to the multidimensional visual perception model presented earlier, in an exercise performed with open eyes and with enough light for the physical vision to work, the intra-physical and extraphysical visual perceptions are blended and presented as a single overlapped image to the observer.

Most of the time, the paravision perception is faded when compared to the physical one. In some cases, however, paravision can be stronger than physical vision, causing very interesting effects. Seeing *through* physical objects and experiencing objects temporarily disappearing in front of you are two examples. Both happen when the extraphysical vision became so strong that it overshadows your *physical* vision.

For the extraphysical vision to predominate like this, you normally need a deeper level of relaxation. I recall a practical class I was teaching when, in the beginning of an exercise, I could see one of the participants, Tim, an intraphysical consciousness, very clearly. He was about three yards from me, on the first chair on the left of the hallway that extended in front of me. There was a stack of chairs in the back of the classroom and I could see it reach a few inches above Tim's head from where I was sitting.

As the practical exercise developed, I started to see his aura, some movements of energy in the classroom, and the presence of an extraphysical consciousness in a far corner of the room, which are typical perceptions in this kind of exercise.

What called my attention is that at some point I could see *through* Tim's head, as if his head disappeared. I could clearly see the rest of his body up to his shoulder. The neck and head were completely invisible and I could see the stack of chairs in the background. The phenomenon lasted long enough for me to count the number of chairs I could see above his shoulder, seven, and whether or not I could see the complete front edge of those chairs that would normally be partially hidden by his head. I was able to verify the perception later, as there was no physical way to see the complete front edge of seven chairs from where I was sitting. I could only see two, the top ones that were above his head. The remaining ones were partially covered by his head and neck.

This experience illustrates one of two types of "disap-pearance" during clairvoyance exercises. In the example above, clairvoyance tuning made it possible to see through something physical, the head of the participant that turned "invisible" or transparent. This first type of disappearance is rarer and the deeper level of relaxation and the attention focused on clair-voyance for a longer period of time is normally what "switches off" the physical vision. From that point *all* visual perception comes from paravision.

The second type is a lot more common and happens when tuning is locked in the bioenergy dimension, and all you can see are the energies in front of you, as if you were surrounded by a thick fog. In practical exercises people would often tell me "you disappeared" when I was a few yards in front of them. The accurate description, however, is that they could only see the energetic dimension, which was between the observer and me, and the perception of those energies was so clear that nothing else could be seen.

Color Perception

This is a point that often generates a lot of debate. There are several books that present tables and meanings for several colors. The issue is that both personal experience and accounts from perceptions of independent researchers show that colors are not necessarily universal indicators of characteristics (such as the state of health or personality) of the person being observed.

The psychosphere, or personal energetic field, is very dynamic. One thought can change the shape, color, and movement of the visible part of the psyschosphere, or aura. Moving your energies through your own will power can also change the color and shape of your aura. Those changes can be quite fast. This is to say that any color observed would be a sample of how the aura looks at that particular moment, and not a weighted average of the state of the energies of that individual. To evaluate someone based on a single observation or color would be equivalent to say that a person is *always* dressed up when seeing his wedding picture.

Moreover, we know that the consciousness is complex and ten or fifteen colors would hardly capture such complexity. Trying to fit people in a pallet with a few colors is as superficial as measuring a football player solely based on his capacity to run or aerobic capacity. We know that a good player needs several additional qualities beyond those two to be successful. Some aspects that could linked to the player's performance can be intricate, such as motivation and willingness to cooperate.

I have also witnessed two observers seeing two different colors in the aura of a third person being observed, at the exact same time, in the same experiment. This is connected to clairvoyance tuning. Sabrina and John, in a clairvoyance class, could see green and blue respectively, in the aura of the instructor they were looking at, during the entire exercise. In a case like this, how would you interpret the color?

There is also the cultural aspect, where influence from society can bring specific meaning to colors and bring a certain bias to the analysis. Red, for example, can be a reference to danger or sensuality in occidental cultures, while in the Chinese culture it is an imperial color. A person seeing the red color could associate it with "passion" or "power," depending on which culture has influenced her.

We often find it hard to describe nuances and textures of what we see in physical terms. There are experimenters that see a lot of detail in the energy and extraphysical events, but fail to detect and describe the specifics for lack of vocabulary or experience.

The complexity around color observation and the results of analyzing hundreds of clairvoyance accounts suggest that the most productive approach is to create an *individual* map of general information conveyed by colors. In other words, it seems to be more productive that each experimenter attempts to identify relative meanings and patterns and associate them to colors, based on the accumulation of personal experiences.

The experimenter can validate such patterns and meanings through other forms of parapsychism, for instance, psychometry or intuition, or by verifying with intraphysical means, the information obtained via clairvoyance.

For example, suppose that you see the color green in the aura of some people, but not in all of them. Supposed as well that you create the hypothesis that green is correlated to energies charged with a more rational, less emotional pattern. You could then try to observe the aura of people that you know to have this higher frequency of rational manifestation, or a lower frequency of emotional manifestation, and verify if in those cases you see green more frequently. The accumulation of experiences would then validate – or not – the hypothesis.

Local Clairvoyance

To better characterize this type of clairvoyance, we will explore several examples selected among the most common types of perception of extraphysical dimensions. The accounts that follow are primarily from practical clairvoyance workshops.

Initial Extraphysical Perception

A sensation of variation in lighting conditions is a common perception during a clairvoyance exercise. In the physical dimension, lights remain dimmed, with constant brightness, but the experimenter sensation is that it became significantly brighter or darker at certain parts of the exercise.

Some can have the perception of seeing everything as we would see in negative photographic film, those used before digital cameras came around.

Having the sensation that the person you are looking at is closer or farther away, and that the distance changes during the exercise is also common. Similarly, the distance between the side walls, or how high the ceiling is, can apparently change. Other apparent changes in the physical space are also possible.

Those experiences happen, usually, when the extraphysical visual perception (psychosoma) starts to blend with the physical visual perception (soma, eyes), causing distortions in how the physical dimension is perceived. Those effects can be quite intriguing.

I recall a "field course," a type of immersion workshop with intense energy activity, where three members of the support crew that were observing the epicenter-instructor entering the hall, noticed it looked like he was over eight feet tall, when this instructor is, in reality, well below six feet tall. The crew was about fifteen yards from this instructor, and in low light condi-tions this could be dismissed as an illusion if the difference perceived was not so large.

The observers were in a deeper relaxation state but alert, a condition conducive to clairvoyance. The instructor later validated the perception, as he noticed a very tall extraphysical consciousness energetically connected to him at the moment of the observation. The hypothesis is that all three crew members have seen the combination of the physical image of the instructor with the extraphysical image of the very tall extraphysical consciousness. The result was a distortion in the height of the intraphysical person observed, making him look taller.

In a different city and date, but also in a field course, I had another one of those blended experiences. I was working as part of the support team and sitting in a chair on the south side of a large ballroom. The floor was covered by a carpet with an intricate pattern in burgundy, black, green, and beige. As I looked down for a few moments I started to see very gentle waves, about one or two inches high, which made the floor look malleable.

The waves were coming from my right to my left and progressively became taller, up to a point where they reached about three inches. At this point I could move my eyes and my head and the undulation would not stop, which confirmed to me that clairvoyance was active and "locked in" to that particular area of the energetic dimension.

A few moments afterwards I was able to control clairvoyance so that I could see the waves (physical + extraphysical) or only the static floor (physical), depending on the will command I selected. I continued to experiment with different things and was able to tune in on the waves and afterwards move my arms, torso and legs while maintaining both physical and extraphysical perception.

Energetic Dimension

The energetic dimension is usually perceived as a mist, cloud, fog, or white smoke, comparable to the image you see through an airplane window as it goes through a cloud.

In a survey applied to participants of clairvoyance workshops 44 percent of the participants had this kind of perception.

Another energetic dimension perception happens when you look upwards to the sky, or to the horizon, in places with lots of energies from nature. The paraperceptions could be described as bright spots of about a third of an inch in diameter, about ten yards away from you, moving at random, as in a cloud of mosquitos, except that the dots would be bright and lively. The "Aeroenergy Technique" creates the ideal conditions for this type of perception.

It is possible to see your own aura, from the inside out, when you are inside of your physical body. You can try this when lying in your bed, taking advantage of a deeper relaxation that can be achieved, and lower lighting conditions, which will help in the process.

Extraphysical Dimension, Indirect Perception

An extraphysical consciousness can be detected indirectly when we see their energies or energies that they move as part of their manifestation.

I recall several occasions when I saw a group of bright luminous spots moving in random fashion, similar to the energetic dimension perception presented earlier, but concentrated in an area the size of a human face. This perception indicates the presence of a conscex in that location.

In a spontaneous clairvoyance experience that happened in the hypnopompic state (between being awake and asleep, as I was waking up), I was lying down on a sofa when I perceived a very bright shape between two long bracken plants, about four yards away. This very bright light had the shape of a cat's eye, measured about eight inches high by four inches wide, and was floating in the air, about five feet from the floor. I was about twelve at the time and could not find an explanation for what I had seen. Several years later, as I learned about extraphysical dimensions and parapsychic phenomena I understood the event as an energetic manifestation of an extraphysical consciousness. There was someone there, an extraphysical person.

In this case, I detected the extraphysical person in the extraphysical dimension not because I was able to reach that dimension and see her psychosoma. Instead, I was able to see the manifestation of the energy from that consciousness in the energetic dimension.

In some cases, the energy manifestation you see takes the shape of the psychosoma of the conscex, taking you "closer" to the extraphysical dimension. Towards the end of the music video "Thank You," from Alanis Morissette, the visual effect used when she interacts with a semi-transparent being in a store resembles this kind of perception.

I was able to see the shape of the psychosoma of a conscex in motion while working on a clairvoyance exercise based on energetic coupling, another example of indirect access to the extraphysical dimension. For a few seconds I was able to see this conscex walking across the room, with the shape and movement of the bright energies around his psychosoma making it possible for me to discern arms, legs, torso and head clearly.

Extraphysical Dimension, Direct Perception

Seeing people and objects directly, from the extraphysical dimension is very interesting, but something that happens less frequently.

In some cases, the extraphysical consciousness can be seen with such clarity that the observer may take it as physical perception. It is more frequent, however, that the psychosoma will be perceived as semi-transparent, or with faded colors.

The account below is from Kathleen, and illustrates how the clairvoyance perception can be very clear:

I was in a party at a friend's house. At some point I entered an empty room where I found a large mirror with an elaborate frame, one of those used in classic decoration style and is set off the floor, leaning against the wall. I was alone in that room and stopped in front of the mirror where I stared at my own face for a few minutes. After that I could see, along with my own reflected image, two more people about a yard away, behind me. I could see both very clearly, in detail. Both had a neutral expression. When I turned around to see who those people were, they vanished!

The movement of the physical body probably interrupted the altered state of consciousness relaxation that triggered the spontaneous clairvoyance experience for Kathleen.

Another account of direct perception, this one from a practical clairvoyance exercise:

I saw an older man, perhaps forty years old, dressed with beige colors, khaki trousers, a simple dress shirt, rolled up sleeves, no beard, a type of skinny face, brown skin... The hair was big on the top side, similar to a ducktail haircut. It   looked as if he was from the 70s... He was walking from there...to this side of the room, slowly but in a determined, deliberate way, as if he was in the middle of a task. The psychosoma was semitransparent when he was far, but as I started to notice the details and tried to see the colors, the impression was that he turned more opaque, more visible. I could also see that his energies interacted with Elaine's [a participant, conscin] as he passed by her, as if a type of wind.

This account described details of an extraphysical consciousness, with face and clothing characteristics, indicating direct access to extraphysical dimension. Had the observer been projected, he would see that consciounsess with the same level of detail. The experiment indicates a minor tuning adjustment, as the change in opacity changed during the observation.

In the same exercise, the other student – Elaine – confirmed that she felt an extraphysical consciousness in the place and approximate time described by the observer. She was unable to see the conscex in that occasion, however. Two additional participants of the exercise also detected the extraphysical consciousness in the same route, but with different modes of perception: they only saw energy movement in that area.

The combined perception of energy movement and seeing the psychosoma can also happen.

A great visual effect that resembles this aspect as well as a progressive change in tuning is a scene from the movie *Contact*, directed by Robert Zemeckis in 1997, and adapted from the novel of the same name written by the North American scientist Carl Sagan. There is a scene in this movie when the scientist Eleanor Arroway (Ellie), played by actor Jodie Foster, meets her father on a beach, in a place that seems to be a distant planet.

In the beginning of Ellie's perception, she only sees energies moving in the air. Gradually, those energies take the shape of someone walking towards her, then the shape of a semi-transparent man can be discerned, and, finally, she can see that the man was her father when he was a few yards away. If we use this as an analogy and if her father was a conscex, we could say that, at first, she had an indirect perception of his psychosoma when she saw energies only, and later had a direct perception from the extraphysical dimension when she saw the psychosoma of her father.

Clairvoyance and Materialization

Seeing an extraphysical consciousness through clairvoyance is different from seeing the materialized psychosoma of an extraphysical consciousness. In the case of materialization there is no need for clairvoyance since the manifestation is based on very dense energies, typically involving ectoplasm, making the psychosoma physically visible, i.e., it reflects physical light. Any person or object that materialized, therefore, can be seen with physical eyes, not requiring parapsychism.

Clairvoyance and Semi-Materialization

Not all visual perception of the extraphysical dimension fall under materialization *or* clairvoyance, there are gradations for both phenomena and the possibility of both being combined.

Clairvoyance can be facilitated by semi-materialization, in the cases when the extraphysical consciousness "goes" towards the intraphysical dimension, partially materializing through the densification of her psychosoma, while the intraphysical observer "goes" towards the extraphysical dimension by means of paravision.

The jargon for when clairvoyance is facilitated by semi-materialization is the "fifty-fifty" effect. The combination of phenomena can happen spontaneously, in an everyday setting, as well as in structured exercises.

Travelling Clairvoyance

In this phenomenon, the observer uses *extraphysical* means to see something in the *intraphysical* dimension that is happening in a distant place or out of reach from the physical vision of the observer.

Travelling clairvoyance (TC), or remote viewing, seems to work from a type of stretching of the psychosoma and/or the energosoma all the way to the observed target. It allows the observer to capture the remote images as if she was in the remote location.

Some experimenters manage to verbally describe or draw the scenes they see while the phenomenon is happening, which suggests that TC does not require the full disconnection of the psychosoma.

Since TC allows an experimenter to obtain information about targets that are not physically accessible, a few projects were developed during the cold war era aimed at developing new modes of espionage. Though the intention of such experiments is definitely questionable from the cosmoethics standpoint, some of the research programs produced consistent results and led to the development of new methodologies and protocols.

A recent example of this kind of program is Stargate, which was conducted in the United States. This program remained secret for several years and was described in the book *Remote Viewing Secrets* by one of its participant-researchers, Joseph McMoneagle. Several participants produced high level of detail of various pre-selected targets reached through remote viewing.

Travelling clairvoyance can be combined with energy reading techniques (psychometry) and mental target techniques to obtain information about missing people and remote places. This is a phenomenon that can happen spontaneously during parapsychic development exercises or in states of deeper relaxation.

The Image Target Research Project – ITRP, conducted by researcher Patricia Sousa and I, invited people from around the world to attempt to see an image displayed in a computer monitor across several days. The image was picked at random from a bank of images, and could be a photo of an object, person, landscape, or a simple geometric shape.

Participants did not have a chance to see the images beforehand, and should report results every morning on a website. A different image was selected at random every night from a bank of 190.

The most common type of observations would describe the shape of the objects in the picture, colors, or association of ideas. An example of such observation, from Operator 6 of the ITRP, is as follows:

Image A: Blue Waste Paper Basket

I saw a black square! It was a quick glance, a flash, immediately before I left my bed in the morning.

Although the target was not a black square, the general shape of the image and the darker color of the object are aligned with the description of the experimenter.

Several of the accounts examined indicate that consistent and accurate description of the images requires significant training from the participant.

Although accuracy was not consistent in this Travelling Clairvoyance experiment, at times, the resulting description included very specific characteristics of the target and even detailed drawings. Some detailed descriptions make it very hard to support the argument of a "lucky guess."

An example of this kind of observation, also from the ITRP, from Operator 23:

Image B: Wooden Horse and Teddy Bears

I saw a shelf with a plush teddy bear. The bear was not exactly brown; it was dark yellow or beige. The teddy bear looked a bit sad, with its head tilted to one side and a ribbon around the neck. There were other things on the shelf as well, but I could not see more detail.

In this case, the operator was more than two thousand miles from the target, had information about the address, and only knew that pictures or geometric forms would be displayed on a computer monitor.

Chapter 5

Classifications and Examples

About Classification

Identifying categories is often one of the first strategies used when studying a phenomenon with a scientific approach. Collecting and classifying specimens and observations – and also thoughts and experiences – are present throughout the history of scientific discovery.

Classifications can be done in several ways. Cars, for example, can be classified based on main function (sports, sedan, pick-up truck) or color (red, green, black). The objective when presenting several classifications of clairvoyance is to outline the possible variations of the phenomenon. The classifications can also help to shed light or provide a different understanding of past experiences with extraphysical vision.

Knowing more about clairvoyance can also prevent the sudden interruption of an experience that often comes with the surprise when we see something we did not expect. The more we know about the possibilities, the more we will approach everything we see with productive and serene curiosity.

Learning more about the possible types of observation can also motivate you to expand your perceptions. For instance, if you hear about a type of agglomeration of energies you have never seen, but someone else has, you could look for that type of perception in your next experiment. Another possibility is that perhaps you have seen that agglomeration of energies before, but only recognized it when you heard a detailed description from someone else.

Dimensions: Energetic, Extraphysical

As presented in Chapter 4, Clairvoyance Characteristics,

paravision enables us to perceive images from the energetic dimension and from the extraphysical dimension.

Descriptions of visual perception from the energetic dimension typically involve the words fog, mist, colors, and bright spots. Direct perception of the extraphysical dimension typically involves the description of conscexes.

Image Position

1. Combined with the physical perception

In the majority of local clairvoyance accounts, the experimenter sees the extraphysical images superimposed with the images seen with the physical eyes.

Nelson, one of the participants of a clairvoyance exercise reported the following:

> I had my eyes opened and was looking at the instructor [sitting about two meters away]. Despite the reduced lighting I could see his face and body pretty clearly... Also the objects around him, the white board in the background and the framed pictures on the left.
>
> As I relaxed [further] I noticed that my energosoma became a bit more loose, and I started to see a disc, or an accumulation of light, in a flattened round shape, of about eight inches in diameter, in the upper side of his head, towards the back, more or less in the position of a halo.
>
> [...] the interesting aspect is that I saw this bright disc of energies and at the same time I could clearly see the face of the instructor, exactly how I saw it in the beginning of the exercise.

The account above describes the experience of seeing with clairvoyance and physical vision at the same time: both the face of the instructor and other elements of the physical dimension were visible along with the extraphysical energies of the coronochakra of the instructor.

Figure 8: Combined Visual Perception

Another phenomenon where the physical visual perception is combined with another source is the retrocognition (past life recall). In such cases, the experimenter sees content from her holomemory play out as if it was happening in the surrounding physical environment.

2. Screen in front of you

This type of perception is at times called "mental screen," and the screen can open up slowly, or appear at once in front of you, and begin to display images of what is happening somewhere else or in an extraphysical dimension.

Figure 9: Screen in Front of You

Observing events in a screen is often reported in experiments of travelling clairvoyance. Both retrocognition and precognition (premonition) can also be experienced in this manner. The differentiation of the source of the images and how to identify when it is clairvoyance will be discussed in Chapter 9, Clairvoyance and Other Phenomena.

3. See through an opening

While applying a technique in a practical class, Johnathan had a spontaneous travelling clairvoyance. The objective of the class and the technique was to produce an out-of-body experience; however, the account illustrates this mode of image perception very well:

I recovered lucidity and realized everything was dark around me. I could only see a bright dot in front of me. Little by little this dot was increasing in size and when it was approximately 12 inches in diameter I was able to see the other side. It was as if a thin black wall, about as thick as a plywood sheet was right in front of me, with a big round hole in the middle... This hole continued to widen until it was approximately this size [about 10 feet].

During the whole time I could see the black edges of the opening and could control the direction I was looking at. My field of vision was not completely open [...]. I was seeing the kitchen in my house and I could see my father preparing a salsa that he normally prepares for us to eat with nachos. This felt a bit odd since my father normally does not do this kind of thing on Saturday, he always leaves it for Sunday. The images were from the kitchen, but I could hear people talking in the parking lot [next to the classroom] and a crack in the bookshelf [in the classroom]... It took me a while to understand that the sounds were not from the kitchen, but as I am reviewing the experience now it is clear that those sounds were from the classroom.

Johnathan was able to verify his travelling clairvoyance experience as he later arrived at home and learned that his father did, in fact, prepared the salsa on that Saturday, and could not think of a reason for the exception. The experience caused a great, positive impact on him.

Seeing through an opening is often reported in travelling clairvoyance experiences. In the account presented above, the perception of noises and voices happened through physical senses, while the visual perception from a place several miles away was received through travelling clairvoyance.

The concurrent physical perception is what indicates that the phenomenon was travelling clairvoyance. If Johnathan were outside of his body, in an astral projection, he would not have heard the noises from the environment where his physical body was located.

4. Inside your head, with your eyes open

In this mode of perception, you see something outside your physical field of vision, for example, behind you, while seeing the physical dimension in front of you at the same time. It is rarer to hear accounts of this type of paravision, and a bit more attention to detail and skill would be required to separate it from other forms of visual experience.

I had this type of perception in a three-day immersion course, where a field of energies is created that often has the effect of bringing the physical and extraphysical dimensions "closer."

This field of energies has an instructor as an epicenter, typically someone that worked as an instructor for parapsychic development for several years and who connects with an extraphysical team in order to establishes the field. The epicenter is the "root" or point of intraphysical connection for the field of energies.

As part of the support team for that course, my role was to help the participants that got close to the epicenter to receive an energization. I was focused on this task, although I could feel several energetic sensations, as it is frequent in this kind of energy work.

One of the clear sensations I had, and a persistent one, was of the presence of an extraphysical consciousness, standing about five feet from my right shoulder. I felt this for at least fifteen minutes, but stayed focused on the task for which I was responsible. The epicenter was about ten feet to my left. During those fifteen minutes I was feeling the presence of the conscex I had no visual perception of him, but the perception of his presence was strong.

Suddenly, when I turned my head to my left, I could see the complete image of this conscex, inside my head. I was looking away from the conscex and he was outside my physical field of vision. It was as if I had an "additional eye" on my right temple, and that I was seeing this man with this "additional eye." The man I saw noticed that I saw him and looked in my direction, and smiled, as if acknowledging the "visual contact."

Clairvoyance came spontaneously and I could see him in perfect detail. It was a man in his sixties, very well dressed in a light brown suit, tailored to perfection.

I was also able to read some characteristics of his pattern of thoughts and sentiments (holothosene), a strong and serene pattern, with a certain dose of optimism and good humor, giving the impression that he had accumulated good evolutionary results through experience, in many lives.

As I turned my head towards this consciouness, I stopped seeing him. It took me about fifteen seconds to recover a bit of the extraphysical vision and to see the energy contour around him as well as an aggregate of luminous spots around the area where his face was. At this point, however, I could not see the extraphysical dimension directly.

The clairvoyance "inside your head" can also be used to see the extraphysical companion of someone intraphysical you are speaking with. In cases like this, the image of the extraphysical consciousness will flash inside your head. Although the time you "see" the image inside your head tends to be very short, the clarity and level of detail of the image tends to be very high.

What normally triggers this type of perception is a more relaxed state combined with an energetic connection with the person you are observing. Due to the fleeting nature of this phenomenon, you need a good level of acuity with your perceptions (in general) in order to identify this kind of clairvoyance. It is also important to have good mental discipline to avoid personal biases and imagination to "fill in the blanks" when your short-term memory fails to record the clairvoyance flash in detail.

Time: Always Simultaneous

Clairvoyance is the perception of the present, from physical or extraphysical dimensions. It is important to establish this time reference to differentiate clairvoyance from retrocognition and precognition, which work through different mechanisms.

Precognition means to receive information about something that will happen, or is likely to happen, in the future. This phenomenon involves the mentalsoma and it seems to be a kind of conclusion about a large set of variables that become accessible to the experimenter.

Retrocognition, in turn, implies accessing the extraphysical memory we have (holomemory). That is to say it is not a perception, but a retrieval of information stored in holomemory.

We understand that watching a tennis match live is different from watching it from a recording one day after. In this analogy, clairvoyance is equivalent to watching the live event while retrocognition is equivalent to watching the recorded event, some time after it actually happened.

When we see the video recording the day after, the images are coming from the recording, which represents memory in this analogy. Clairvoyance, in turn, is similar to looking at the match directly as it is happening, so it is not related to memory and is, instead, a form of perception.

This topic can cause divergence and even confusion, especially when the approach is more of a mystical one, and when the term "clairvoyance" is used almost as a synonym to parapsychism in general.

We will explore more differences between clairvoyance, precognition, and retrocognition in the chapter "Clairvoyance and Other Phenomena."

Movement: Static or Dynamic
Both local clairvoyance and travelling clairvoyance can present images in motion as well as static pictures of extraphysical elements being observed.

Travelling clairvoyance often includes the observation of intraphysical scenes and its inherent motion. It is akin to seeing images on a monitor, transmitted from a camera that is far away.

In local clairvoyance it is typical to perceive movement of some kind, or at least a bit of vibration or "life" as we observe energies.

In some cases, the perception of movement can happen when we see a sequence of static images, something typical in the observation of the outer layer of the aura.

Edward, a participant of one of the classes in Miami, described that while he observed the external part of the aura around the instructor, around five feet from his head, he noticed that it moved constantly. His perception and absence of perception alternated every second. For an instant, he would see the contour of the aura of the instructor and would stop seeing it immediately after, with this cycle repeating several times. The sequence of several images indicated the motion of the external layer of the instructor's aura.

The indirect perception of the extraphysical dimension include movement in the vast majority of times.

Duration: Long, Short, Flash

The length of a clairvoyance perception can vary a lot. There are accounts of individuals that experienced clairvoyance for days in a row. Others experience it as a flash or fraction of a second.

Isabelle, one of the students in Lisbon, reports that she was able to see the auras and energosoma of others for several hours on days she would go for a swim before starting her workday. She attributed this to an overall deeper physical relaxation and unblocking of her energosoma.

In long duration techniques, such as the three-hour physical immobility technique, which involves staying lucid and awake for three hours with no physical movement, clairvoyance can start in the first few minutes and only stop at the end of the experiment. This would allow for several hours of paravision, and experiences could include seeing your own energies, the energies of the environment around you, movement of extraphysical consciousnesses, and many others.

In shorter exercises, clairvoyance normally lasts for minutes, depending on the speed and relaxation control of the experimenter. In the clairvoyance workshop, exercises would normally last around 25 minutes including 10 minutes of relaxation and work with bionenergies. This would allow for about 15 minutes of applying a clairvoyance technique. The typical result in this exercise structure is a period of at least five minutes of clear extraphysical vision.

Chapter 6

Optimizer Factors of Clairvoyance

There are several important factors that need to be observed while applying clairvoyance techniques. Naturally, not all factors are important to everyone and to every level of clairvoyance experience. Changing a small aspect of a procedure or paying more attention to one detail can make a big difference to a person and be absolutely irrelevant for the next. And specific procedures that could help one person trigger her paravision could be detrimental to another.

It is important to keep in mind that optimal conditions help, but are not necessarily required. There are many reports of clairvoyance obtained under apparently unfavorable conditions, so it is difficult to say that factor "A" or "B" constitutes an absolute condition for experiencing extraphysical vision.

For example, Judith reported in a workshop that stressful work conditions would normally trigger her ability to see the auras of her colleagues, when stress is a condition that makes it harder to experience clairvoyance for most. As a general rule, the more negative stress, the less parapsychism, but general rules can fail in specific cases.

It is important, however, to study factors that could make it easier for you to access your paravision, particularly when in the beginning, or until you get to the point where you learn how to operate the "switch" that turns clairvoyance "on". After you manage to find and learn how to control this "switch," you can try in less than optimal conditions.

For some, the clairvoyance experiences may end up limited to a known and predictable set of experiences for a long period of time. One of the ways to break through such pattern is to examine the concepts in this chapter and see which variable can be changed.

Lucid Relaxation

We can divide the ability to relax in two main components: the **physical** relaxation and the **mental** relaxation.

Physical Relaxation

Physical relaxation is mainly connected to muscle relation, a condition that facilitates the expansion of the energosoma and, in turn, allows for a bit more mobility of the psychosoma, as you begin to exit the condition of total alignment of the holosoma.

Muscles of your face, lower back, and sometimes arms, can be tense without you noticing it, making you "more intraphysical" and connected to the perceptions from your physical body. Muscular tension can be associated to stress or anxiety, and one can be more or less lucid to how much both are connected. Muscles may be tense due to lack of stretching and even because of prolonged exposure to cold temperatures.

Physical body relaxation normally causes a gentle reduction in heartbeat, breathing pace, and, in some cases, a minor reduction of blood pressure and body temperature.

Although physical relaxation is not strictly necessary for clairvoyance, this factor contributes the most for parapsychic perceptions in general, particularly to those who are starting in this field.

And what level of relaxation is needed to facilitate the process? The ideal level is when the experimenter can barely feel the physical body, to the point a floating sensation starts to set in.

In order to reach such level of relaxation it is necessary that you choose a comfortable position. As a reference, you should not feel any discomfort whatsoever in the first three minutes. Examples of minor discomfort that can limit your relaxation: a belt that is too tight, pressure in the arms due to how they are supported by the armrest, a fold in your clothing that becomes perceptible as it restricts the blood flow slightly, pressure in any region of the physical body due to its position, constant skin sensation as it is in contact with specific materials, and so on.

While applying a technique in a seated position, the ideal is to keep your back straight and your head well positioned to minimize the effort to keep it still and aligned with the rest of your body. Some prefer to rest their head in a pillow or to use a chair with a high back, but this is generally not needed.

One of the indications that the person is more deeply relaxed is the absence of physical body movement. It is natural to adjust our position during the first few minutes of a clairvoyance exercise, and move our hands, feet, or head in that process. If such adjustments persist throughout the exercise, however, the constant movement tends to decelerate the relaxation and energosoma expansion, which creates a less favorable condition for clairvoyance.

The ability to relax with lucidity can be learned and can be controlled at will. With time and practice, relaxing becomes second nature, like breathing or walking.

I had an experience that underscored how physical relaxation can be controlled at will. When a doctor was measuring my blood pressure in a routine medical check and said, "Relax," before taking the measurement, I was distracted, but took the suggestion literally and did not notice that, issuing a "mental command," I relaxed so much that the pressure reading read abnormally low. The doctor was surprised and informed me about the reading. As I noticed that perhaps I had relaxed too deeply, I requested a new measurement. This time I was careful to maintain the relaxation at "normal" level, and the second reading was normal.

The speed of relaxation is also something to which we need to pay attention. Ideally, we should relax in a controlled and progressive way so it is easier to stay lucid in the process.

A person that did not sleep enough for several days will relax very quickly, but the lucidity will probably be lost very early in the process. If the person is sleepy and has her eyes closed, she is very likely to see only oneiric images, which are associated with dreaming and the hypnagogic state. This is to say that it is better to have slept well in the days that you apply clairvoyance techniques.

Another sleep-related recommendation is to train the relaxation in a chair, and not in a recliner, comfortable sofa, or in a bed. If you are sitting on a chair and lose control of the relaxation process, or if your relaxation progresses too quickly, the loss of control of the muscles that hold your head straight will cause your head to tilt quickly. The reflex of bringing your head back up gives you the opportunity of taking control of the process and continue with more lucidity.

Caffeine

Because it is a psychoactive stimulant, caffeine can make the relaxation harder for some. The influence varies from person to person. In some cases, the experimenter does not fully appreciate the influence of this substance, and how it affects the extra-physical vision. Thus, it is worthwhile to eliminate all forms of caffeine intake for two weeks, for example, and to see if this makes relaxation easier during your clairvoyance experiments.

It is important to highlight that caffeine is added to several sodas, chocolate, and to some sweets. Some types of tea may have the same stimulant effect. We may be ingesting the same amount of caffeine contained in two or three espressos within a few hours depending on the combination of food and beverages selected.

The same logic applies to other stimulants like taurine and guarana: it is always a good idea to verify the effect they have in the quality and depth of your relaxation.

Physical Exercise

It is known that moderate physical exercise can improve physical and energetic health and bring several benefits. Walking at a fast pace for thirty minutes, three times a week is an example of a moderate exercise routine.

Exercising can help significantly, both in the general case of parapsychic development and in the particular case of clairvoyance development. There are at least two reasons for that: first, because endorphin naturally produced will help you achieve a deeper level of muscular relaxation, and second, because exercising will naturally help you unwind and improve your mental relaxation.

It is not uncommon for people to incorrectly assess their own level of relaxation. Many figure they have relaxed enough when that is not the case. Because of that, frequent physical exercise will bring a third contribution: to allow the person to experience deeper relaxation states, bringing new references for comparison and showing what is possible in terms of relaxation to the experimenter.

The type, intensity, and duration of the exercise are also relevant to reach the relaxation level that will promote psychic experiences. Intense exercises, like weight lifting or running, can bring several benefits to the physical body, but could provoke a temporary "deeper intraphysicalization" of the consciousness. Intense exercises can also produce adrenaline or to speed up metabolism for several hours after the exercise is over, causing an adverse effect to physical relaxation.

Fernando, a student I met on one of the courses, experienced this very directly while participating in a series of four weekends where practical parapsychic development techniques were being applied. He was progressing well in the extraphysical perceptions until the third weekend. On the fourth weekend he decided to go for a run, at a faster pace, in the sun, in the typical 100 Fahrenheit (38 Celsius) and 90 percent humidity of a summer in Miami. After showering and getting ready, he headed to the projective technique class. The result was a clear contrast from previous classes: he was unable to relax in the first half of the class, and went straight to sleep in the second half, with no lucidity.

What Fernando experienced is typical of exercises that demand more from the physical body. In this case, the strenuous run made him "more intraphysical," making it harder to perceive the extraphysical, and to relax in a controlled way. He was too alert in the first half of the exercised, then "crashed," going quickly into a deep relaxation state with complete lucidity loss. This is not to say that those exercises are incompatible with parapsychic development: the key here is timing. It would be more effective to wait for the next day, or to try mild exercises, such as walking, in the days preceding the parapsychic experiment.

Going back to the analogy of overlapping screens, the importance of relaxation is that it makes the images on the physical screen less bright. As we relax and "slow down" the physical body, our physical perception becomes less intense, which in turn gives us a better chance to discern the images from the clairvoyance screen. In other words, the intensity of the image we see with our paraeyes becomes more similar to the intensity of the images we see with our physical eyes.

Mental Relaxation

One of the main inhibitors of clairvoyance is anxiety. Most of us are exposed to the immediate, hyperactive, hyper-caffeinated, multi-tasked culture where everything needs to be done now, quickly, instantly. It may be hard to understand and assess how much of this culture has been absorbed and how much of it we consider "normal."

Clairvoyance requires several characteristics that are opposite to this culture, characteristics that include a state of relaxed alertness and lucid openness. I often quip in clairvoyance classes that clairvoyance rhymes with patience.

Anxiety can come in several forms and have different origins. One of the most common roots of anxiety is the fear of extraphysical consciousnesses. There are cases like Luisa's who would say that she wanted very much to develop clairvoyance, but at the same time was afraid of spirits (conscexes). Luisa would unconsciously sabotage her own progress in clairvoyance exercises. Dozens of energy exercises were needed for her to get used to the sensations from her own energosoma so that she would be at ease when perceiving the energies of an extraphysical consciousness. It took another dozen exercises for her to see the face of an extraphysical consciousness without major stress.

In this example, clairvoyance worked as a tool to overcome the fear from other dimensions, and from other forms of parapsychic ability. As she accumulated experience with the energetic dimension, and later with clairvoyance, Luisa slowly reduced the fear she had of out-of-body experiences. As she collected extraphysical interactions while in full control of the experience, the confidence in her own parapsychic ability increased. With less anxiety about what she could perceive, she was able to relax further and experience the extraphysical dimension more directly.

Anxiety can also be less evident as an issue in some cases. An experimenter can be very serene during the exercise up to the point where he starts to see something new, or something clearly different from what he is used to, and then interrupt the experience, startled. In this context, fear produces a "knee-jerk" reaction that reconnects him to the physical body, quickly switching off his paravision.

A key goal in parapsychic development is to replace fear with a state of "bold serenity." This state would allow all perceptions to be received in a posture of healthy curiosity, a spirit of scientific inquiry and sense of discovery. This can be achieved through working with energy techniques along with clairvoyance experiments.

Self-Blocking

Complexity is plenty when discussing self-imposed limitations on perception. Even excess scrutiny during an experiment can interrupt your perceptions. Questioning is a very good thing when reflecting about an experience. However, when done constantly while trying to experience paravision, or as soon as you start seeing extraphysical things, can cause a sudden interruption of the parapsychic process.

It is generally better to be open during an experiment and make objective mental notes describing your perceptions, leaving the detailed analysis for after the experiment. Even when writing down notes about what you have experienced it is usually more productive to separate the description of your perception from your interpretation of it.

Having said that, the impulse to confirm the perception *while* seeing it is natural, and can be done in a non-disruptive way as you accumulate experience and have better control of the phenomenon.

A beginner may squint as soon as he starts seeing the psychosphere of someone else, just to "check if it is really there," and immediately stop seeing it. Squinting, eye movement, or head movement tend to cause a reconnection of the psychosoma and to interrupt your paravision, especially when done right after its onset.

The ideal posture is to take a "journalistic" approach, allow the experience to "flow," and see up to which point your extraphysical vision will go, and relaxing further and staying serene. After the end of the experience you can transfer your mental notes to paper, or to a computer file, and proceed to the critical analysis.

In future opportunities you could go through the same cycle once more, trying to get answers to the questions you raised during the analysis period of past experiments.

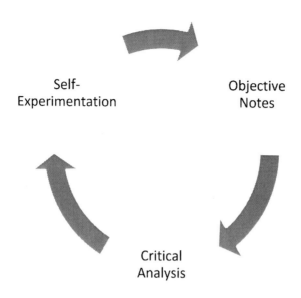

Figure 10: Self-Experimentation Learning Cycle

Blocking your own clairvoyance can be even more subtle and complex when considering the consequences of confirming the existence of extraphysical dimensions with personal experiences.

Seeing extraphysical consciousnesses and elements of extra-physical dimensions, for example, will inevitably make us think about life after death. Though most people *believe* in life after death, in a religious or non-religious way, a relatively small number have direct experiences with extraphysical people. In other words, many accept the idea of life after death, but few contacted spirits that already died, in a way that was not ambiguous. And the confirmation of continuity beyond this physical life through first-hand experiences can bring deep questioning, possibly including changes in priorities, decisions and values. It invites us to question what we are doing with the time and resources we have in our life. Sometimes the hardest part is not to know what we *have* to do, but what we should *stop* doing.

Although such questioning and possible changes in

perspective are inherently positive, they constitute a threat, in practice, to the comfort zone of the vast majority of people. Clairvoyance, in this context, can become something of a threat to the *status quo*. This is why, in some cases, the experimenter believes he *wants* to see, declares that he is ready and has no fear, applies effort, but subconsciously remains blocked and sees nothing beyond the physical dimension. Beyond the superficial display of willingness, he actually feels better when clairvoyance does not work or remains at a basic level, in a way that it can be more easily dismissed as optical illusion or something along those lines. The less clairvoyance, the less urgency or need to leave the comfort zone.

Moving Your Head

We have already established that the best strategy to facilitate physical relaxation and to place your psychosoma slightly out of alignment is to avoid physical body movement.

Avoiding moving your head is what helps the most in this context: with expanded energies around your head and your parahead slightly out of alignment, you will produce a better condition to start seeing with your paraeyes.

A small adjustment in the leg position is usually not as problematic as a small adjustment of your head, muscles in your face, or around your eyes.

Eye Movement

Even with the physical body completely still you may end up moving your eyes while applying a clairvoyance technique. This can be an issue depending on when this happens in the experiment, on the state of alignment of your psychosoma, and whether or not your clairvoyance is "locked in" to the specific dimension and space you are observing.

Eye movement can happen voluntarily or involuntarily. We may deliberately look at something a few inches to the right of what we were looking at before, making a lucid movement based on will power, or unconsciously move our eyes quickly, scanning the face of another person, in an instinctive procedure that allows us to cover a larger area with the center of our retina and get a clearer picture.

The quick, small, and involuntary eye movement is called "saccade" and it tends to happen when we try to fixate our gaze at a particular point for a longer period. A widely accepted hypothesis is that the receptor cells in our retina become less responsive with a steady stimulus. The involuntary movement would "refresh" the image on the retina and make our physical vision more clear.

The whole point here is to learn how to look without eye movement for a certain period of time, and use this strategy during clairvoyance exercises.

The conscious part is easy to resolve: all you need to do is to look at a fixed spot on the wall or on the person you are observing during the clairvoyance exercise.

In order to control the spontaneous quick involuntary eye movements, however, you will need a bit more self-observation

Figure 11: Rotating Snakes, by Akiyoshi Kitaoka and Hiroshi Ashida

and training. If you have never seen those lateral eye movements, ask someone to look at a specific spot down a hallway, for example, and pay attention to their eyes while they do it.

Another way to detect spontaneous eye movements is to look at the picture on the previous page, which was designed by Akiyoshi Kitaoka and Hiroshi Ashida, and aim to produce the illusion of movement. The image has elements with a specific pattern of step-changes in luminance.

The illusion is usually stronger on the peripheral vision, so as you are reading a line that is an inch or two from the picture the effect will be stronger. You will also tend to notice more movement as you move your eyes around.

There is nothing to worry if you do not see this illusion – some simply do not and, if this is your case, you are already looking in the best way to facilitate clairvoyance, so you can skip over to the next topic.

If you do see movement, the challenge is to learn how to stop it. If you look at one of the black dots in the picture steadily, and relax mentally, the illusion can stop. Seeing the illusion in this exercise means that you are moving your eyes, a static image means that you are looking the way you should look during a clairvoyance exercise. Try to record your sensations and observe what you do, or "how you are looking" when the image stops. The goal of the exercise is for you to learn how to look steadily and avoid conscious or unconscious eye movements.

The reason to avoid eye movement is that such movement seem to trigger the brain to "reprocess" the visual stimulus from your eyes. In the overlapping screens analogy, this would be equivalent to making the screen with physical images brighter, which in turn would make it harder to detect the more subtle images in the paravision screen.

Blinking is something necessary to our physical vision as it keeps the surface of our eyes clean and lubricated. The movement of our eyelids and brief cessation of physical vision also triggers the "reprocessing" described above. Stoppping blinking completely for a long period of time would be something hard to do – and possibly unhealthy depending on how long we would keep our eyes open.

The account below is from Giuseppe, who reported that every time he blinked during the exercise his clairvoyance would switch off:

> *About three minutes into the exercise I started to see the outline of the energosoma around [the instructor]. This outline would never disappear and, little by little, I was able to identify the coronochakra and the outline of your aura, about five feet from you…*
>
> *The problem was that every time I blinked part of the coronochakra and the aura would disappear. It was as if I would take a couple of steps back [in the perception]. After some time without blinking I could see both [through clairvoyance].*

A frequent question at this point is "should I, then, not blink?" The answer is "no," because your eyes would eventually feel dry to the point of causing discomfort and reconnection. The most effective strategy to manage blinking can vary from person to person.

Some prefer not to blink for longer periods, when comparing to the time between blinks during the normal waking state. And, when they blink, they do so in a very gentle way, trying to move the eyelid only and nothing else. The counter-example here is the person that moves even the cheeks while blinking, often without noticing it, which can get in the way of your paravision during an experiment. It is worthwhile watching yourself blinking in the mirror while blinking in the most gentle way you can and evaluating how much effort you apply to this action.

Another way of minimizing the effect of blinking is to keep your eyes partially open, but without obstructing your vision.

This should also be done with the least amount of effort possible. In fact, when you relax, the natural position of your eyelids will naturally be a bit lower.

With partially open eyes you will also reduce the evaporation surface of your eyes, so it will take longer to get to a point where you need to blink and rehydrate.

It is also important to pay attention to heating and air conditioning, as both can dry up the air and make our eyes dry. Fans and constant air currents have the same effect, so it would be ideal if those are not present.

Another strategy to manage blinking is to establish a constant, deliberate blinking pace. You would, for example, blink every five seconds, in a constant pace. The interference will still be there, but the fact that it is constant could help it to be less distracting. A similar strategy is used for breathing, where a constant, monotonous rhythm can help to get to a point where breathing is "automatic" and interferes less in the relaxation process.

A third possible strategy is to reduce the speed of the eyelid movement, so that the total time between having your eyes open and completely shut is about four times slower than it would normally be.

Managing blinking applies mainly when we are trying to get clairvoyance "started." Once you get it going and it is "locked in" to a certain dimension, blinking will not interfere and may even be used to adjust your intraphysical viewing, as long as you do it slowly and stay focused on the extraphysical perception. This might sound contradictory with the guideline provided earlier "if you blink, clairvoyance goes away," but this is a matter of timing, pace, and intensity of the blinking process.

Now, suppose you see something that matches the description of an aura. If after five seconds (timing) seeing this image you want to adjust your physical vision to get further evidence that the perception is real, you can blink in a very gentle way (intensity), and verify if the aura is still there after you blink. If you blink with more intensity, to the point you move several muscles on your face, the perception of the aura will probably go away, but not because it was not there in the first place. It was because the physical movement caused the vehicles to reconnect and align fully, interrupting your paravision.

The recommendation is to try the different strategies described and see which one is more suitable to your particular case.

Illumination

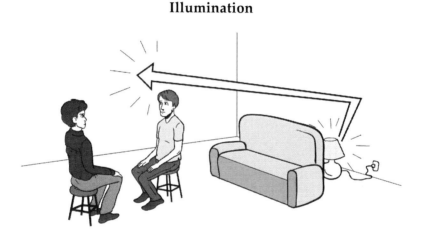

Figure 12: Indirect Illumination

Another way to reduce the intensity of our physical visual stimuli is to reduce the illumination of the place we are in. This is a basic technique that applies to almost every clairvoyance experiment.

Reduced lighting can contribute in the beginning of your training and when the objective is to perceive the more subtle areas of the aura, or to make a direct observation of the extraphysical dimension.

An indirect form of lighting should always be favored, which means that the light will bounce at least once before reaching the object we are observing or our eyes. This usually means hiding the light source behind something, so that the light will be reflected by the ceiling and walls before entering our field of vision. As a general rule, lighting should be placed behind the observer-experimenter. If the observed-experimenter cannot see the light directly, even better. The picture on the previous page shows an example of setup that could work well.

One of the conditions that normally get in the way in a clairvoyance exercise is when there is natural light behind the person we are looking at. A window behind the person we are looking at, during a day session, can make it harder to perceive the energetic dimension and the extraphysical dimension.

Diffuse lighting also helps, as it will not generate shadows with high-contrast edges. The issue with marked shadows is that the dark-light contrast in the edge of the shadow can be a strong physical stimulus in itself and interfere with more subtle extraphysical perceptions.

Naturally, aspects of illumination are one of those variables that helps more when you are starting the learning process. We should not think that low lighting is a pre-condition for clairvoyance, however, since extraphysical visual perceptions can happen even under direct sunlight.

Physical Vision

Although clairvoyance is independent from physical vision, the majority of the exercises proposed will involve experimentation with open eyes and enough light for your physical vision to work.

In spite of the apparent incoherence, there are at least three reasons to use physical vision *along with* paravision. The first one is that, with eyes open, we have an objective reference of what we are seeing. This will make it easier to differentiate what is a physical image and what is not in a clairvoyance exercise. You will have a baseline from your physical perception and will be able to identify changes from that baseline.

Second, we have a conditioning that is part of our personal paradigm that tells us that we stop seeing if we close our eyes. This is a conditioning reinforced during all the time you have been alive in this life, and from all your previous lives, something fundamental in our biology: we need physical light to reach our retina to be able to see anything.

Although it is technically possible for clairvoyance to work when you have your eyes closed, it would be necessary to overcome this very strong clause from your personal paradigm. You would essentially have to ignore the suggestion of your biology in order to see with your paravision.

The third reason might be more pragmatic in the context of parapsychic development and helps to identify more clearly specific phenomena that you can experience in the various altered states of consciousness. It is a lot easier to eliminate images from the hypnagogic state if you have your eyes open, for example. It would be very hard for an adult in normal conditions to enter the hypnagogic state with his eyes open. With eyes closed, most would start seeing oneiric images from the hypnagogic states after about ten minutes of relaxation.

Therefore, a clairvoyance experiment done with closed eyes requires more experience, vocabulary, and sharper acuity when collecting and classifying perceptions. It would be harder to determine the source of the images you have seen, and ultimately to determine if your experience involved clairvoyance or not. With your eyes open, all this complexity goes away.

It is well known that the hypnagogic state itself can conduct the experimenter to several altered states of consciousness and various phenomena, including clairvoyance. The intention here is not to completely exclude the hypnagogic from your parapsychic development, but simply to put it aside temporarily in order to identify clairvoyance in a more isolated way, independently from oneiric forms of visual experience.

Naturally, having your eyes open brings its own obstacles, like the physical body movement and blinking. However, we can overcome those obstacles quickly through objective procedures.

Finding the Switch

When someone asks me what exactly I do to trigger my paravision, the answer is "it is a will command." I know of procedures and techniques that helped me to find and operate this imaginary switch that turns it on. Most of the time I do not need techniques or procedures, I just "will" to start seeing the energetic dimension, for example.

Thinking about it, I reckon it would be as hard to explain what I am doing when I am typing. I cannot name the muscles and joints involved in moving my fingers and pressing keys in the right order to produce this text. But I know how to type.

Since "will to see" and "a will power command" are abstract, and explaining things that we cannot demonstrate or point to a diagram and explain, the proposition is to use simple techniques to produce basic clairvoyance experiences and, from there, learn how to switch it on and off at will. After that, we can progressively develop more control of specific aspects of the phenomenon, like tuning into a specific dimension, through self-experimentation and accumulation of experiences.

We will work with aspects of physical vision in order to find the clairvoyance switch. The logic here is to work with subjective commands over something we know how to control (physical vision), and have objective means to verify if the command worked. The familiarity with changing your physical perception with a subjective command based on your will power will pave the way to do the same with extraphysical perception, with your paravision.

Closed Circuit of Energies and Vibrational State

The Closed Circuit of Energies (CCE) consists of moving energies from your head to your feet, moving your own energies up and down inside your own energosoma in a cyclic movement, using your will power, and increasing the speed of your energies to the point it triggers a vibrational state.

In a simple approach, we can say that one of the key objectives of this technique is to unblock and activate chakras and your energetic system. You can also reach the Vibrational State (VS), where your entire energy body vibrates in a pleasant sensation, indicating energetic balance and homeostasis.

Reaching the Vibrational State is ideal for clairvoyance exercises because it clearly indicates that your chakras are unblocked, a condition that is helpful for parapsychic development in general.

Even if you don't reach a vibrational state through the CCE technique, the exercise works as a "warm up" for the energosoma, creating better conditions for your clairvoyance exercise. The CCE will also provide you with opportunities to identify energy sensations and will help you to get started in the relaxation process.

A summary of the steps in this technique is as follows:

1. Accumulate some of your own energies in your head.
2. Move this accumulated energy downwards, slowly, through your body, until it reaches your feet. Your objective is to make the energy go through all parts of the energosoma and all cells of your physical body.
3. When your energies reach your feet, move this accumulation of energies in the opposite direction, towards your head, establishing a continuous cycle, form your head to your feet, then from your feet to your head.
4. Keep repeating this movement. Try to identify regions where you feel the energies flowing through, and regions where you do not feel those energies, or where the energies disperse or go around. Those sensations may

indicate energetic blockages. If you identify blocked areas, try to focus your attention on those areas as you move energies through. The goal is to activate the blocked areas by focusing on pushing energy through, to the point your energies flow up and down without impediments.

5. At the point where the energies move evenly through the energosoma and without blockages, start to accelerate the energies, increasing the pace of the movement up and down up to the point it spontaneously triggers a vibration sensation of your whole energosoma. When you reach the vibrational state you will feel the energies vibrating inside and outside your body, a pleasant sensation that indicates energetic homeostasis.

The Vibrational State also helps to interrupt the energetic coupling between the experimenter and other consciousnesses, intraphysical or extraphysical. This is a factor that makes the VS so important in the development of parapsychism and in promoting healthy experiences.

Beyond that, mastering the VS can bring a series of benefits in terms of consciousness development. For this reason, practically every course and publication in conscientiology includes references to the VS, and I recommend reading the books in the section "Conscientiology References."

The mastery of CCE and VS normally requires a certain amount of time and persistence and trying the techniques in a deeper relaxation state makes it easier to discern the sensations from the energy body.

Chakras and Clairvoyance
The closed circuit of energies promotes the unblocking of chakras and tends to induce a slight expansion of energies. This exercise can work as a preparation or warm up period for clairvoyance techniques.

Although the frontochakra is the chakra that is mostly connected to clairvoyance, having *all* chakras unblocked often helps *more* in the clairvoyance development process.

I have seen several cases in paravision workshops of individuals with a very active frontochakra, often due to frequent intellectual activity, but with the cardiochakra quite blocked. This combination resulted in a *lower* paravision ability, lower even than the ability of someone else that had both chakras in a "neutral" state (not exactly active, but not blocked).

As a general rule I can say that it is smarter to look for a condition where *all* chakras are reasonably unblocked first. Activating your frontochakra will bring a lot more results once you manage to keep the other chakras unblocked for longer periods of time.

Figure 13: Frontochakra

Exteriorization of Energies

Another basic exercise we can do with our energosoma is to exteriorize energies. This technique consists of donating your own energies to the environment around you, to expand your field of energies, and to densify the energies in the field in which you are participating.

Exteriorization can help in at least two aspects in your

parapsychic experimentation: activating a specific chakra and in densifying the field of energies.

You can activate a chakra by focusing the exteriorization of energies on a single chakra and keeping the energy flowing in pulses for a few minutes. One of the preparation techniques proposed later in this book consists of activating the frontochakra with this procedure.

The exteriorization of energies can also promote the unblocking of a specific chakra. We know that unblocking the energosoma helps in clairvoyance development and that the Closed Circuit of Energies can help in detecting and unblocking our energetic body. Exteriorizing energies can have the same unblocking effect, when focused on the area that we intend to unblock.

We can also create better conditions to experience clairvoyance by exteriorizing energies to the room we are in and densifying the field of energies around the participants of the experiment. A denser field is easier to see through paravision and, because of that, many clairvoyance sessions start with an exteriorization of energies.

There are a large number of energy techniques and exercises that can be performed with various objectives; however, we will keep those out of the scope of this book and limit our description to a small set of fundamental exercises. The closed circuit of energies, the vibrational state, and the exteriorization of energies are the ones more closely connected to clairvoyance. For those who would like to know more about energies, I recommend the section "Conscientiological Bibliography" at the end of this book.

Peripheral Vision

Our field of vision can be divided in two areas: the central vision and the peripheral vision. The peripheral area starts at approximately seven degrees of arc from the center of your field of vision.

The outer area of our retina, responsible for receiving the images from the peripheral area of our vision has less cells and provide less detail about what we are observing, while the central area has a higher concentration of receptor cells and provide us with more detail, to the point we can, for example, read.

If you look straight to a single word at the top of this page and stare at this word only, without moving your eyes, you may notice that the words at the bottom of the page are less sharp and impossible to read. This is because those words at the bottom of the page are reaching the outer area of your retina, where there are less receptor cells. In fact, it may even be hard to discern clearly lines of the text at the bottom of the page while looking at the top line of the same page, though you can see that there is text there.

For clairvoyance, this lack of physical detail in the periphery can actually help: since we are receiving "less visual input" in this area, perhaps we can more easily detect the extraphysical input there. In the multiple screen model presented earlier, this is equivalent to saying that the edges of the physical screen are less bright than the center. This would make the obfuscation of paravision effect milder, which means receiving extraphysical images in the periphery of your vision would be easier.

The account from Marcus illustrates this aspect:

I was reading a book in the kitchen, at night. My wife and kids were already in bed sleeping and the house was in almost absolute silence. All I could hear was the humming of the fridge and a few cars driving thought a street nearby. I was engaged in the reading and could see the kitchen door from the corner of my eye. This door led to the hallway that was dark at the time with the lights off.

After about thirty minutes of reading, I clearly saw someone walking quickly across the hallway. I thought, could it be Juliana, my daughter? I then realized I did not hear footsteps on the wooden floor… I stood up and walked to my daughter's bedroom and verified she was sleeping. Then looked at the master bedroom, [where] my wife was also asleep. I [went back to the kitchen] and resumed my reading. In less than ten minutes I saw the extraphysical consciousness going through the hallway again. This time I remembered not to look directly. I stopped reading, kept my eyes on the book, but directed my attention to the door. Less than a minute later I could see the outline of the psychosoma of the conscex. She had stopped at the door and was looking towards me. The energy I sensed from that person was calm, as from a curious child trying to understand my presence and why I was so focused on reading.

Clairvoyance was triggered spontaneously in this account, and was detected in the peripheral vision, as Marcus was looking at a book.

The instinctive reaction in a case like this would be to look directly at what is calling our attention in the peripheral vision, a movement that would probably interrupt the clairvoyance perception. This is why the idea of looking at one place but focusing your attention in another place will be referenced in a few of the preparation exercises and techniques. One of the goals is to learn to resist the impulse of looking directly at anything that calls our attention. We want to allow some time for the tuning of our paravision to "lock in," which can take from a few seconds to, perhaps, a bit over a minute. After our tuning is locked in, we can look directly and take the time to better examine the extraphysical perception.

In lots of cases we see energies, chakras, and extraphysical consciousnesses precisely where we are **not** looking. In workshops where participants are sitting in rows, it is common for those in the back rows to see the auras of participants in the rows in front of them while trying to see the aura of the instructor in front of the class. Those perceptions often surprise the participants, as they were not expecting to see anything extraphysical on those areas.

The Use of Glasses and Contact Lenses

As an extraphysical perception, paravision does not require the use of corrective lenses. It is, however, recommended that you wear your prescribed glasses or lenses during a clairvoyance exercise in order to provide a baseline image, a reference in the form of a clear physical image that can be easily contrasted with anything extraphysical you see.

This principle applies in particular to nearsighted people (myopia) and to exercises aimed at seeing energies around someone that is a few meters away. It would be harder to identify extraphysical perceptions if everything was blurred. Having said that, and going back to the point that there are usually exceptions to any generalization, I can recall at least one account of a person with more than five degrees of myopia that had the preference to practice exercises without corrective lenses.

Between glasses and contact lenses and in my experience with both, I prefer glasses, particularly in exercises with the objective of seeing someone else's aura. For the everyday life, however, I prefer contact lenses because the entire field of vision is corrected, allowing me to detect clairvoyance perceptions in the edges of my peripheral vision more easily.

For me, contact lenses also seem to allow for longer periods without blinking, but if I have my eyes open for too long the lenses can dry up and fold the next time I blink. Eyeglasses can present limitations in techniques that use peripheral vision and observation of something at a short distance if you wear glasses with small lenses.

In order to minimize the dryness issue, I have used eye drops, those specific to contact lenses, right before the exercise. I would also keep my head tilted with my eyes looking up and blink a couple of times to allow the eye drop fluid to spread evenly.

Daily Training

As with any other form of parapsychism, the principle of "the more attempts, the better" also works with clairvoyance. This might seem obvious at first, but since we are immersed in a culture of immediate results, it is expected that some people will give up after just a few attempts, using a very limited set of techniques – a strategy unlikely to produce results – and incorrectly conclude that clairvoyance does not exist or that they cannot do it.

Our day-to-day routine will offer plenty of opportunities to develop our parapsychic ability. By applying common sense and some discretion, we can try to see the auras of the people around us and do small experiments of clairvoyance under different lighting conditions, colors, and types of energy. All of that is possible, for example, while in line at the supermarket, in meetings, on the bus, public transport, at school, and so on.

We should always work on a CCE technique before and after the attempts, trying to install the vibrational state to maintain our energetic balance.

The only restriction here is while driving – or performing an activity with equivalent attention requirements and risk characteristics – in which case it is better **not** to try any type of parapsychism. Driving requires *physical* vision and an attentive waking state so trying to relax and get your holosoma out of alignment would not be safe. I strongly advise against trying clairvoyance while driving or equivalent circumstance, since the relaxation you will be trying to reach could make you fall asleep or take your attention away from where it should be – on the road. This would create a high-risk condition for you and for others.

Field Density

To exteriorize bioenergies before a clairvoyance exercise can help densify the field of energies in the room you are in. As a general rule, it is easier to see energies that are more dense than it is to see more subtle ones.

We do not have control over this specific factor all the time, but it is good to keep the density of the energy field in mind if you are trying to create better conditions to experiment with your paravision.

I have been in exercises where everyone did everything "right" in terms of procedure and did not see anything. Ten or twenty minutes later, in the next exercise and applying the same procedure, the same experimenters had several perceptions because the field of energies was denser compared to the field in the previous exercise.

The subject of field of energies is somewhat complex, but one thing we can say, based on experiential data, is that physical movement gets in the way of creating and maintaining a field.

Even when the experimenter is deeply relaxed and not moving, the movement of another person can interfere in the field conditions and in this experimenter's paravision. In group exercises, therefore, the ideal is that all involved try to avoid moving as much as possible.

Intentions, *Cosmoethics*

In a simplified way, we can define cosmoethics as a set of principles, relative conduct guidelines, and values that are the most productive for consciousnesses. Cosmoethics goes beyond the physical manifestation of the soma. To think destructively towards someone, for example, is *anti*cosmoethical, since the negative energies of the person that is thinking will be sent to the person that is the target of those thoughts, an act of thosene-based aggression.

Waldo Viera, the researcher that proposed the term, presents the following definition in the treatise *Homo sapiens reurbanisatus:*

Cosmoethics (cosmo + ethics) is the specialty of conscientiology applied to the multidimensional study of ethics or reflection of cosmic morals, defining the consciential holomaturity, placed beyond intraphysical social morals or any morals presented with any human label, a maximum emotional and moral discernment, stemming from the intimacy of the microuniverse of each consciousness.

Since clairvoyance goes beyond purely physical perception, it is coherent to think about it in terms of cosmoethics when developing this parapsychic ability. We must extend ethics beyond the basic human understanding to assess what is productive and what is not when seeing through paravision. We will explore clairvoyance aspects from a cosmoethical perspective in the next sections, below.

Action and Reaction

It would be great if the popular belief that "if you do something bad the spirits will take the gift of clairvoyance from you." Multidimensional reality is not that simple. One concept that can help you a lot in understanding why cosmoethics is fundamental in parapsychic development is to think in terms of action and reaction.

If the intention of the experimenter is not good, the individual holothosene will be affected. The change will evoke extraphysical people with similar intentions who, in turn, can bring negative influence to the experimenter. This simple statement opens a wider discussion about relations between intraphysical consciousnesses and extraphysical consciousnesses, with a key concept being the fact that one's intention selects extraphysical companions.

In fact, a similar logic applies to intraphysical life: if someone is dedicated to fraud and money laundering, he will end up choosing a specific circle of acquaintances and friends. Due to the nature of the activities he is involved in, he would more likely to be threatened physically and have his life at risk.

In this extreme, illustrative example, the choice of laundering money removed at least one aspect of individual freedom: as the illicit activity develops, more and more secrets have to be kept by those involved. Each participant has the power to harm others with what they know, and could, for example, use it for blackmail.

Using the logic applied to this scenario to something more commonly found, and thinking about the extraphysical consequences: If Joe decides to obtain information through clairvoyance in order to manipulate someone, his energies will align with extraphysical consciousnesses that, in some level, accept manipulation as an option. In other words, the tendency is that his extraphysical companions will have a lower cosmoethical standard. This is to say that those companions would not hesitate, if they deem useful, to manipulate Joe. Those conscexes can more easily connect energetically to Joe due to the affinity in thinking, and Joe will lose at least one aspect of his individual freedom as he is subject to manipulation from the extraphysical companions.

Cosmoethical behavior attracts cosmoethical behavior, and the opposite is also true. The saying "what goes around comes around" is the popular version of this logic. There is no punishment or sentence, only cause and consequence. The immaturity of the consciousness involved often makes matters worse. In this context, to try to decide and act with higher cosmoethical standards is more than a moral stance: it is a sign of evolutionary intelligence and multidimensional awareness.

Quality of intention also drives clairvoyance tuning. Non-cosmoethical actions and intentions will tend to limit the experience to denser portions of the extraphysical dimension.

Energetic coupling facilitates clairvoyance, particularly facial clairvoyance, which happens more easily when there is affinity, rapport, or something in common, imprinted in the energies, with the extraphysical consciousness you see. Therefore, our pattern of thoughts and sentiments (holothosene) will determine whether or not we can see a more evolved consciousness during an exercise. The pattern of energies is a reflection of the cosmoethical code of conduct. A consciousness that is advanced in terms of evolution, has an advanced understanding and practice of cosmoethics. To make it easier to see an advanced consciousness, the observer would have to reach a holothosene that is aligned with this higher level of cosmoethics. That is to say that the overall level of cosmoethics of the experimenter determines the evolutionary level range that will be more easily observable during a clairvoyance exercise.

Another key aspect is that anticosmoethical actions and intentions interrupt the energetic connection with helpers, who can help a lot in the parapsychic development process. This help can come in many ways: telepathy, triggering intuitions and insights, unblocking the energosoma, activating a particular chakra, and activating parapsychism in general.

So it is not that the helpers will block the experimenter's psychic ability if he drifts into anticosmoethical behavior: they step away to avoid participating in it and, in doing so, withdraw the support that activated the parapsychism in the first place.

The quality of our intentions is inevitably reflected in the field of energies around us so it is not enough to have an intellectual understanding of cosmoethics. Our thoughts, decisions, and actions need to *be* cosmoethical in order to imprint a more productive pattern in our energies.

I heard hundreds of cases related to cosmoethics while leading workshops, but the story Clarice told me during a break in one of the classes was one of the clearer examples of cause-effect connected parapsychism interruption. She had a business partner that got interested in clairvoyance and was progressing with increasingly interesting experiences. At some point she had the ill-inspired idea of trying to use remote viewing to spy on her main business competitor to try to figure out their strategy. She thought this would give her own business an advantage. In the very first attempt her parapsychic performance was abruptly reduced. Her helpers stepped away as soon as she committed to the anticosmoethical route.

Helpers and Intruders

The nature of interaction with extraphysical companions can be better understood if we divide the results of the interaction in two categories: helpers and intruders.

In this two-category split, a helper is the extraphysical consciousness dedicated to assistance and that has lucidity and cosmoethics as the main characteristics. The fundamental characteristic of the helper's intention is to help in what is possible and cosmoethical towards the best outcome to all consciousnesses, having the multiple dimensions, multiple lives, and consciousness evolution in perspective.

The intruder effect is the opposite, focused on direct or indirect anticosmoethical actions that influence the consciousness energetically connected to him. Intruders often act based on ignorance about cause and effect, lack of lucidity, egocentrism, personal interest, and pathological emotions. Intruder actions reduce lucidity, tend to oppose individual freedom of thinking and not to respect free will.

There is also a category of intruder called "blind guide." In some cases, the blind guide can help or give strength to an intraphysical consciousness that is energetically connected to him, however, the lack of lucidity and cosmoethical principles delays the evolution of both. The blind guide will also operate as an intruder in important moments and often justify anticosmoethical means with his own interpretation of "a good outcome."

A blind guide can act like an old friend that is irrationally conservative and opposed to any change of habit you propose, even positive ones, and even those that could represent a very significant step forward in your evolution, one that was five lives overdue, for example.

Certain blind guides are opposed to parapsychic development due to concerns with the potential renewals that might be triggered by parapsychic experiences. Others try promote a religious or mystical interpretation of parapsychic experiences. This is why self-knowledge is so important, and particularly studying your own holothosene.

All thought and sentiment actions – including the true intention of the experimenter – are always public from the extraphysical viewpoint. It is possible to say something and think something else in a purely intraphysical exchange. For extraphysical consciousness, however, it is possible to "read" the thought and true intention of the experimenter that becomes evident in the bioenergies. In this context, the premise that "nobody saw it" is invalid if you consider multiple dimensions.

It is important, therefore, to understand the pattern of personal actions, thoughts, stances, and intentions, since those will, ultimately, determine the quality of your energies and, as a consequence, the quality of our extraphysical companions.

To seek a more cosmoethical pattern of thoughts and sentiments helps in clairvoyance development for at least two reasons: (1) the more advanced pattern of extraphysical companions will promote positive and educational experiences and (2) the presence of helpers will increase the possibility of "sponsored" parapsychism. Helpers can conduct the experimenter to advanced experiences, densify the field of energies, or unblock a specific chakra, for example.

Deassimilation and Discernment

We have already established that we can get into an energetic coupling with other people in day-to-day situations. The depth of the energetic interaction can vary in everyday scenarios; for example, a "hello" that lasts two seconds does not usually result in a deep energetic interaction. A handshake followed by a two-minute chat, in comparison, would mean a bit deeper energetic exchange. A thirty-minute talk with a friend, about subjects of common interest, would naturally open the possibility of a greater energetic contact and probably an energetic coupling.

Some exercises with energies for parapsychic development, including the facial clairvoyance technique (explained in Chapter 8, "Clairvoyance Techniques"), can result in a very intense energetic contact.

If, on one hand, the energetic coupling can produce very interesting clairvoyance experiences, on the other, it can make the influence of the energies of the person with whom we had contact linger, sometimes for several hours after the exercise. This influence (or energetic assimilation) can be active or neutral, positive or negative, desirable or not, healthier or more patho-logical. This is in line with what we explored earlier, in the context of interactions with helpers and intruders.

In this context, there are two important aspects to consider for exercises with energy (including clairvoyance techniques) with two or more participants. The first one is the choice of those people (discernment) and the second one is the deassimilation of energies.

As for the first aspect, it is important to utilize – and sometimes to improve – the capacity of choosing (discernment) and to look for groups and people with a pattern of energies that are productive and balanced. Try to sharpen your ability to evaluate people and situations around you continuously, paying attention to intuitions and indications that something is not comfortable for you, or not productive or helpful energetically, but at the same time avoiding an extreme form of "purism," that may limit your experiences.

A whole book could be written about this, but, as a brief reference, we can ask, will the energies I feel during the exercise improve my lucidity? Is the pattern more of consolation or more toward clarifying and understanding what is happening? Is the atmosphere more of mystical awe or focused on comprehension and learning? More of healthy self-scrutiny or distorted by big egos? More altruistic or selfish? More or less sectarian? More or less manipulative? When in contact with those energies, do I feel well, confident, and serene? Do the energies and experiences facilitate self-knowledge and reaching my potential?

Sometimes, when I present the recommendation of being selective with whom we apply energetic techniques, I am asked if this is not elitism and if it would be better to always accept *any* person. Other times, I am asked if it is better to do all exercises alone, avoiding a more direct energetic contact with other people.

These are two extremes that can be compared with something familiar to all of us: inviting someone to our house. You probably apply certain criteria about whom you invite to your home, meaning you do not have an open-door-to-anyone policy. In contrast, if we *never* have a guest in our house, maybe this means that we are relatively distant from friends and relatives, and maybe we would be missing out on the benefits of being closer to other people.

This is precisely where personal discernment comes in: what is more important in my case, in my context? Having *more* or *fewer* guests? What types of interactions and situations would I consider good and productive? What kinds would I like to avoid?

The interactions that I describe, intraphysical or extraphysical, have a point in common: the consciousness. It is important to keep in perspective that extraphysical consciousnesses, helpers, blind guides, and intruders are all **consciousnesses**. This is what makes guest-in-the-house analogy so suitable. A lot of the common sense we apply to *intra*physical consciousnesses can be applied to *extra*physical consciousnesses as well.

Desoma (discarding the human body, death) does not transform the consciousness into the ultimately pure form of good or absolute evil. The configuration of his or her capacities, interests, characteristics, and objectives – productive or destructive – do not change instantaneously nor automatically because of death.

In this context, it is definitely better to develop our parapsychism than to stay in multidimensional ignorance. We find more or less the same "types" of consciousnesses in the intraphysical and the extraphysical dimension, with varying levels of cosmoethics. The consciousnesses that we will evoke (call with energy) or filter out depend on our holothosene, actions, intentions, affinities, or, in short, our level of cosmoethics.

About the second aspect, deassimilation, one solution is to master the CCE technique and the vibrational state, as described previously.

The vibrational state promotes energetic deassimilation, the cleansing of your energetic field, and removes undesired energetic remnants that you might have picked up during the energetic interaction.

This technique can also work to balance the individual holothosene before a clairvoyance exercise. If we have just arrived from work, for example, bringing worries from that environment, a CCE can help us deassimilate energies related to those issues. This would in turn reduce the possibility that those energies – and related extraphysical consciousnesses – would interfere with the exercise.

In summary, the two recommendations for any parapsychic-development exercise that involve other people are as follows: first, pay attention to the choice of those people, and second, apply the CCE technique to get in and out of the process with "clean" energies. The goal is to be able to deassimilate energetically after contacts and after coupling with any consciousness, intra- or extraphysical.

The subject of relationships between consciousnesses and cosmoethics is extremely interesting, complex, and difficult to summarize in just a few paragraphs, so I would recommend the conscientiological bibliography for more information on such themes.

Chapter 7

Preparation Exercises

There is a series of basic abilities that are important for clairvoyance development. Relaxation, ability to concentrate, and work with energies are some of the abilities addressed in previous chapters.

We can split the preparation exercises presented in this chapter into two categories: energosoma and control of physical perception.

The main objective of the exercises in the energosoma category is to create a condition in which your energies can flow without major blockages, in a way that your chakras are "open" and "active." The looseness and expansion of energosoma also allows a higher degree of movement of the psychosoma, a condition that makes it easier to identify perceptions from that vehicle, including clairvoyance.

To feel your own energies while applying techniques is also an important step. The objective perception of your own energy body will increase the confidence on your parapsychic perceptions.

As for the category "control of physical perception," the objectives are two-fold. One is to increase lucidity in order to identify and describe nuances (or subtleties) in your physical visual perception. The second is learning how to control the paravision "switch" by conducting experiments with your physical vision and trying to control certain aspects of it.

I normally use an analogy to better illustrate what I mean by nuances. We can think of the difference between a regular coffee consumer and a professional that works every day evaluating the quality, aroma, and taste of a variety of beans from multiple places.

For the common consumer, coffee might have two categories: good and bad. The professional, on the other hand, is able to identify aspects such as acidity, body, aroma, and flavor, in several intensities and with a specific vocabulary for each variable.

Following this analogy, our objective is to develop the identification of specific aspects of physical perception as a preparation to perceive and describe extraphysical nuances of your visual paraperceptions.

Zulmira, a well-travelled professional with extensive cultural background, would describe the aura that she could see as "white" in the first few exercises. After listening to detailed descriptions of other participants in the same workshop – texture, colors, and more – she started to notice some of the subtleties during the next exercises. It is not that she was unable to see those subtleties before; she was simply unaware of what to look for, how to process it, and how to translate those perceptions into words.

Some may decide to skip this chapter and go straight to the clairvoyance techniques chapter. I do not recommend this strategy, especially because those with less patience may reach the incorrect conclusion that a particular technique does not work, even when trying it only one time.

Applying a clairvoyance technique without understanding the phenomenon and without basic abilities to support the process, is equivalent to a purchasing manager trying to get the best price in a negotiation by following a fixed negotiation script and, after the unsuccessful result, saying that the script does not work. Perhaps the script is adequate and brought successful outcomes to many, but it did not work for that purchasing manager because of missing communication skills, a basic ability in that context.

Professional athletes often repeat basic exercises periodically to improve more complex abilities and improve overall performance. Parapsychic development is the same, and the ability to develop complex phenomena like clairvoyance and out-of-body experience is greatly facilitated if you invest some time in basic abilities such as relaxation, energy work, and concentration.

We can also think of the development of basic abilities and complex abilities as a continuous improvement cycle, as represented in the diagram below:

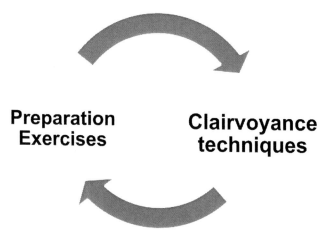

Preparation Exercises   Clairvoyance techniques

Figure 14: Development Cycle for Basic and Complex Psychic Abilities.

The cycle above can also be used to avoid stagnation points or when motivation wanes during your parapsychic development process. I suggest you go through this loop several times and for many basic abilities in order to expand the repertoire of your clairvoyance experiences.

Ideally, we should think like "parapsychic athletes": always trying to prepare for the next series of experiments through deliberate practice. The next sections propose a series of exercises that can be used for this purpose.

Active Versus Passive Clairvoyance Techniques
Clairvoyance techniques can be classified based on whether or not you are "trying to do something" during the observation.

In a Passive Clairvoyance Technique (PCT) you are simply observant, open, waiting for the clairvoyance to start in front of you. You may take steps prior to the observation, such as relaxing or switching the lights on or off, but after that, you are generally just observing. The "window technique," for example, explained in the Acoplamentarium Course by CEAEC in Brazil is a passive technique. The instruction is that the experimenter simply observes, as if seeing through a windowpane, in order to reach clairvoyance.

In an Active Clairvoyance Technique (ACT) you are "doing something" during the observation. The "techniques to change the clairvoyance tuning" in Chapter 4 are ACTs. In the 90/10 technique, for example, you try to concentrate energies in your frontochakra during the clairvoyance observation in order to change the tuning.

Lots of PCTs have been used historically and accounts demonstrate that they do work. However, field experience shows that ACTs usually make a major difference in clairvoyance development. This is particularly important for those who have been working with parapsychism for a few years and have observations within a limited and repetitive repertoire.

By working with ACTs, the experimenter can break the pattern of observation during an exercise. If you find yourself tuned spontaneously to the energetic dimension, for example, without being able to see anything else, an ACT could help you get out of that clairvoyance tuning at will if you wish to do so.

I have heard accounts of people who tuned spontaneously to the energetic dimension and were unable to see anything else during the whole exercise. Had they used an ACT, they would be able to "reset" their clairvoyance and see more, beyond what they had achieved with the passive procedure.

If you have difficulties with blinking or lacrimation, ACTs can also help. Blinking usually does not matter when you are using an active technique, since your attention is focused on operating the ACT itself.

Learning how to work with ACTs can also lead to controlling the clairvoyance tuning at will. This is the most important skill you can develop if you want continuous improvement in your extraphysical vision. Several preparation techniques in this chapter help in the development of this ACT approach.

Control of the Focal Point

An image that is "in focus" is an image that is sharp and not blurry. In optics, a focus is a point where the rays of light from a source converge to, creating a sharp image. In physical vision terms, seeing something in focus means the focal point – where parallel rays of light entering your eyes would converge to – is in our retina.

Our physical eyes adjust the focal point through muscles that change the shape of the lens behind the iris, according to the distance of the object we are looking at. This is what makes the face of someone we are talking to appear sharp, when this person is about two feet away, **or** the leaves of a tree to appear sharp, when that tree is 60 feet behind the person.

The issue is that an object that is two feet away and another 60 feet would require different focal points, or different lenses, in order to produce a sharp image in the retina. This means that we have to choose if the focal point is near, in the face of the person, **or** far, on the leaves of the tree. In normal conditions you cannot have both in focus in this scenario.

Changing the focal point of your eyes is something that happens unconsciously, or "automatically," and it is a physical ability. We can, however, learn how to control this physical ability and indirectly switch on our paravision. A simple technique is to try to focus on a spot that is a few inches before the nose of the person you are looking at. This usually requires a few attempts and can be a bit hard, as we would instinctively focus on the tip of the nose. By trying to do it, though, you can end up triggering a clairvoyance experience.

Several of the techniques presented in this book make a reference to trying to set the focal point on an arbitrary spot. The idea is to control the muscles that change the shape of the lens inside your eyes at will.

Try this as an exercise: Hold this book with your left hand and extend your arm so that the book is held farther from you than the normal reading distance. Now place your right index finger halfway between your eyes and the book. Try to read the text of the book and you will notice your finger out of focus. If you look at your finger, then the text is out of focus.

Now lower your right hand so it is out of the way and you cannot see it anymore. Then try to look at the spot where your index finger was originally, between your eyes and the book. This is harder, as this point is mid-air. It helps if you imagine that there is a mosquito floating in that spot and you are trying to look at it. If you succeed in controlling your physical vision and changing the focal point to be halfway between your eyes and the book the text in the book will be blurry.

As stated before, this is a simple intraphysical ability, but one that can help in several clairvoyance exercises. Learning how to change the focal point at will can also help when we are trying to figure out how to change the tuning of our clairvoyance. The attempt of changing this aspect of physical vision can trigger changes of both positional and dimensional tuning.

Following a Line behind an Object or Person

Ideally, you will work on this exercise with another person. If this is not possible, you can use an object more or less the size and shape of a torso, placed on a desk, or a chair with high back covered by a single-color bed sheet. The background should be a wall painted with a single color, ideally white, ideally smooth.

Draw a straight line on the wall about five inches below the top of the shoulder of the person that is helping you. Do this when she is sitting on a chair so you can better gauge the ideal height of the line. You can draw this line in chalk so it can be easily erased afterwards. The line can also be done with mask tape, which would also be easy to remove after the exercise. Your helper should be sitting about twenty inches from the wall and you should be about six feet away from the wall, also sitting, ideally in a comfortable chair and comfortable position.

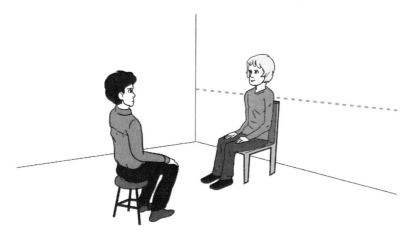

Figure 15: Following a Line behind a Person

Procedure:

1. Close your eyes and take a few deep breaths to relax. Work with energies for a few minutes.

2. Open your eyes and look at a spot on the far left of the line on the wall.

3. Follow the line with your eyes, from left to right, slowly at first, always maintaining the focal point of your physical vision on the wall.

4. At some point the line will be blocked by the body of the person that is helping you. The instinctive reaction will be to adjust the focal point so you can see the person in front of the line in focus. The goal in this exercise is to control this instinct and to keep the focal point on the wall and

stay concentrated on the line, even as your eyes cannot see it as they move across from left to right.

5. When you reach the rightmost end of the line, start moving your eyes from right to left, still following the line. You can repeat the process several times and try to move your eyes at different speeds until you master the ability.

This exercise will help you learn how to control the focal point at will and, more importantly, will help you learn how to slow down or interrupt instinctive reactions from your physical vision. Learning this will help you when you are beginning to see the extraphysical dimension and instinctive reactions make you move your physical eyes, or change focus, which could interrupt your paravision, or change tuning away from what you are interested in seeing.

Another instinctive or automatic reaction is to move your eyes when you detect something moving in the periphery of your field of vision. This is what makes it hard to read an article on one of those websites that have animated advertising on the edge of the text. The movement is constantly calling your attention. The instinct of looking towards something that moves in the periphery of our vision probably helped us way back before modern times: we could quickly assess if the movement came from a predator.

We also tend to look instinctively at something that is on "first plane," close to us. To try to follow a line behind a person will help you control that impulse. A mental frame of mind that is helpful in this exercise is similar to the fraction of a second after someone stops between you and the TV in a critical moment of a movie, when you are deeply interested in what is going to happen.

Another impulse you might have is to look at the face of the person while you are trying to follow the line sitting several inches below. Learning how to manage this impulse can help a lot in facial clairvoyance exercises, where you will be trying to see the face of an extraphysical consciousness superimposed over the face of an intraphysical consciousness. Quite often people interrupt the process when they start to see the extraphysical face because they shift their eyes and try to look directly at the face that is emerging.

Describe and Sketch Your Perceptions

To describe or make a drawing of your extraphysical visual perceptions is an exercise that helps you progress in your clairvoyance development. By attempting to extract more detail from your perceptions you will inevitably raise questions and stimulate your curiosity about specific subtleties. This will, in turn, create a mental frame of mind that will be conducive to seeing more detail in your next experiments.

As an example, we can compare the two accounts below, based on a single extraphysical aspect that was observed by two different people:

1. *"I saw a bright outline around Joanna."*
2. *"I saw the energosoma of Joanna, a bright contour around her whole body, but more intense above the waist. The outline was about an inch thick and was a bit thicker on the left side. The color was not exactly white, but a kind of brightness that had its own light, as opposed to reflected light, it had a bit of a silver hue, as opposed to the blueish hue I often see. The outline did not appear to move, but the thickness and brightness increased when she indicated that she was working with energies."*

Both are descriptions of the energosoma of a third person that is being observed, but with very different level of detail. The person that provides the first description can learn with the account of the second one and, by trying to be more attentive to details in a subsequent exercise, go further in her paravision.

Describing your experience to someone interested and curious in the topic also helps. Questions from someone else make you think about details. It does not matter if you cannot reply; you will always have the next exercise to try to find an answer or to see what was asked. The attempt to try to see something new can help you operate a "switch" in your paravision that you never touched before.

If we talk about our experience with someone that also has clairvoyance perceptions, the exchange is even better. You can compare and validate perceptions. As we try to express subjective experiences we will develop our vocabulary and specific representations of our extraphysical visual perception.

Hyper-acuity in Physical Visual Perception

Due to the possible combinations of color, saturation, and luminance, as well as all other factors at play in a visual observation, there is a tremendous amount of subtlety that can be observed with our physical eyes.

Improving the ability to perceive subtle details has virtually no space in formal education. The majority of people get interested in such themes when required by professional activity, as it is the case with design or various art forms.

Before I became a business partner in a printing company I knew of three types of blue: light blue, regular blue, and dark blue. I did not feel the need for expressing any additional type of blue. As we started to get estimates for industrial printers I started to study color reproduction. I learned that the topic is so complex that there are companies that specialize in determining parameters, equipment, reference sets, and a myriad of techniques to measure and ensure consistent color reproduction. I also learned that there are so many types of blue that some are assigned a number, as names are not practical when the "color space" is too large.

I also learned a number of aspects related to physical vision, details like how "alive" the picture can look when printed on paper that is "brighter" or how the image looks very different after a coat of varnish is applied.

The attempt to refine your physical visual perception can help in refining perceptions in general, including extraphysical ones, as it is the case of clairvoyance. I would recommend studying general color aspects and mechanisms of visual perception both in theory and in practice.

As we develop our perceptive acuity, we may discover details about things that have been "in front of us" for years and were never noticed. This kind of experience can help us soften our reliance on certain personal paradigms related to perception: it shows us that it is possible to look again and see things we have not seen in the first attempt.

Since clairvoyance and other forms of parapsychism consist of expanding perception to extraphysical dimensions, it is important to have a certain degree of flexibility to avoid selfblocking.

Below are some examples of practical self-experimentation exercises that can help in expanding your visual acuity:

1. Observe how colors seem to change with illumination. A red house may appear to be burgundy right after sunset.
2. A day with lower humidity (dry air) allows us to see distant objects as sharper, often making a landscape "more beautiful."
3. Note the apparent difference in hue of two perpendicular walls painted with the same color but with different illumination.
4. Notice when direct and indirect lighting is used and in which environments.
5. Some book covers have a gloss varnish over photos only, with the rest of the page with a matte finish.
6. Study the definitions of luminance, color purity, color

saturation, chroma, and brightness, and look for practical situations where you can see those variables.

Unblocking the Energosoma

For me, working with the energosoma helped me a lot in clairvoyance development. A series of exercises, focused on attempting to reach the vibrational state 20 times a day, practiced over three months, produced significant improvements.

The frontochakra is by far the energy center that people most associate with clairvoyance. "Opening" this chakra would help you develop your extraphysical vision. As explained, however, if that is the only chakra that is unblocked while all others are blocked, you are not in the best condition to trigger your paravision.

This is an account I got from one of the students, Joseph, who had a very active frontochakra but with a very perceptible blockage in his cardiochakra and laryngeochakra. Joseph reported few experiences in the first workshop exercises. At some point, around the third period of practice, he noticed that his cardiochakra was being "worked on" by an extraphysical helper. Right after the pleasant unblocking sensation he started to see the energetic dimension in the room.

Accounts like this one support the hypothesis that the activation of the frontochakra alone do not necessarily predispose clairvoyance, particularly when there are other blockages. Field experience indicates that you are better off when your entire energosoma is evenly unblocked.

Frontochakra: Exteriorize in Pulses

The frontochakra is located approximately at the midpoint between the inner end of our eyebrows, more or less at the edge defined by the bottom of our forehead.

This is the chakra with the largest amount of references in clairvoyance literature. A popular name "third eye" denotes the connection between this chakra and extraphysical vision.

Even though the exact mechanisms that connect the frontochakra and paravision are not known, practical experience shows that it is worthwhile to activate it energetically, especially after reaching a vibrational state, when our energosoma is at an unblocked state.

This exercise aims at activating the frontochakra by exteriorizing pulses of energy through it. You can try this technique while sitting or lying down, ideally in a very low light condition, or in almost total darkness, in a silent space and with your eyes closed.

After about five minutes relaxing and another five minutes working with the closed circuit of energies, the first step is to focus on the frontochakra region. Stay focused on this region for approximately three minutes. Focusing your attention in a specific spot tends to accumulate energies in that area.

The accumulation of energies can bring several sensations: gentle pressure, vibration, pulsation, "electricity," "bubbling," or something like a feather touching the forehead.

As you start to perceive the accumulation of energies, exteriorize a pulse of energies forward, driving your energy with a will command, and try to make your energy reach about three feet from your head. The exteriorization should last between five and ten seconds.

After this first exteriorization, start a cycle where you gather energies in your frontochakra for about ten seconds, then exteriorize those energies in a pulse lasting between five and ten seconds.

Repeat this cycle at least twenty times. Focus all your attention during the exteriorization. After twenty exteriorizations, partially open your eyes, very slowly, without moving your head and while looking forward only, and try to detect the energetic dimension around you.

If you apply this technique in the morning, try to tune into

135

your own aura, to see it from inside and outwards, while looking at a spot in the imaginary line between your eyes and one of your toes.

Nuchalchakra – Frontochakra Hydroenergy Flow

One of the aspects associated with the nuchalchakra is the energetic connection between soma and psychosoma. The process of disengaging the psychosoma from the physical body during an OBE seems to be connected to this nuchalchakra as well.

We aim at unblocking and activating both the nuchalchakra and the frontochakra with this exercise, using the immanent energies present in running water.

The easiest approach is to use your shower for this technique. If you have a shower that sends water at an angle, as the one shown in the picture below, even better. You should be standing and letting the water hit the back of your neck.

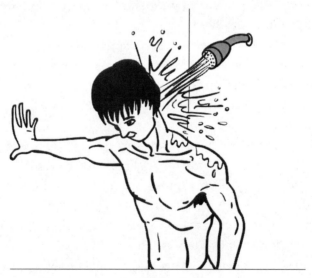

Figure 16: Nuchal-Frontochakra circuit

You may close your eyes to facilitate the relaxation process;

however, in this case, you should have one hand on the side wall to ensure that you will not lose balance.

The idea is to absorb energy from the water through the nuchal chakra and to exteriorize through the frontochakra, creating a stream of energies that goes through your head. You can tilt your head forward a bit and find a comfortable position, where the muscles of your shoulder and neck are more relaxed. Relaxing the neck muscles completely works as well, with your chin getting lowered and closer to your collarbone.

The water should hit the base of your cranium. You may be able to find a "sweet spot" by slowly moving your body an inch or two back and forth, until you feel the energy of the water reaching *into* your head, sometimes all the way to the base of your forehead, from the inside.

A variation in the position is to use a shower stool where you would sit and lean forward, with your arms on the relaxed on the side of your body, so that your torso is supported by your lower back and abdominal muscles.

There is no specific requirement for temperature, although we want to make relaxation easier. Most people would prefer warm water because of that, although colder water seems to make it easier to perceive and connect to the hydroenergy.

Corono-Frontochakra Circuit

This exercise is used as a preparation for facial clairvoyance and it is incorporated in a few curricular courses of many organizations connected to conscientiology.

As in most energy techniques, the first step is to relax the physical body. You can apply this technique sitting, lying down, or even standing up – in this case as long as you take the necessary precautions to keep your balance as you relax.

The second step is to start to exteriorizing your energies through the coronochakra, which is in the upper and posterior part of the head, as indicated in the picture below.

Figure 17: Corono-Frontochakra Circuit

Next, you will absorb energies through the frontochakra as you exteriorize through the coronochakra. Then try to make the energies move in a circle that is half inside your head and half outside your head. This circle goes through both the frontochakra and the coronochakra. Keep your energies going around this path. The flow of energies should activate both chakras and facilitate clairvoyance later on.

When you establish this circuit, you can move the energies slowly at first, and focus on your sensations and on trying to feel the energies in every part of the circuit. This initial phase should last around five minutes. After that you can increase the amount of energies that you are moving around, making the ring of energies stronger, denser, more intense. You can also increase the speed of the energies spinning, but always maintaining the relaxation of your physical body.

The success of this technique can be measured by how active those chakras are after about fifteen minutes. Sensations on the frontochakra and coronochakra can be good indicators of this activation, with common sensations normally described as pressure, vibration, pulsation, "electricity" and "bubbling."

Chapter 8

Clairvoyance Techniques

Persistence

Any exercise designed to develop a particular ability relies on deliberate practice and repetition. No one expects to go through scales in the piano with no mistakes, without a bit of practice. Even if you get it right on the first attempt, it is unlikely that your average will be the same after attempting once versus after attempting one hundred times. The point is to repeat the exercise in order to increase the frequency of good performances.

Clairvoyance is a consciential ability and it is also subject to this rule. Any technique presented in this chapter should be repeated at least ten times before drawing any conclusion about its efficacy. It is recommended that you try in different days and write down any conditions you consider relevant to try to find patterns and hints that can help your development. I usually write down the color of my shirt and the color of the background in classrooms where I teach workshops to assess if there are combinations that increase the type and quantity of perceptions from the students.

Understanding the Process

Techniques are sets of procedures designed to reach an objective. This definition works well for exact sciences, factories, and chemistry. When dealing with parapsychic development techniques, however, the efficacy of a set of procedures cannot be evaluated superficially. It is important to consider the complexity of what you are trying to experience to understand what works in which conditions.

Steps and details of a technique can be planned and detailed to make it easy for anyone to apply it, but this is not to say that clairvoyance techniques are like cake recipes.

For a cake, if the ingredients are within certain parameters, and if we observe aspects like how to mix ingredients, the oven temperature, and allowing the correct time for the baking powder to work, there is a good chance of getting a "reasonable" cake as a product, and perhaps even a tasty one.

For clairvoyance, you would have to address a larger number of variables, with each variable carrying a specific weight depending on your specific profile, condition at the moment of the experiment, and overall skills. This makes it less likely that a list of procedures captures all complexities of the phenomenon. Additionally, we have to keep in mind that one of the "ingredients" is ourselves, consciousnesses, with motivation, level of curiosity, holothosene, extraphysical companions, and mood that can vary significantly from one day to the next.

This is the reason why we present several techniques – or recipes in our analogy. You should experiment with a few, or with all of them, to discover what is more effective for you in each particular context, seeking better results on average. You may also find that combining elements of different techniques is what works best in your case.

A good understanding of the phenomenon is an "ingredient" that should be added to all techniques to increase the chances of success. Thus, once more, I do not recommend this chapter to be the first one you read in this book, since any technique will be less effective when attempted without understanding fundamental clairvoyance concepts.

Aeroenergy Technique

One of the types of immanent energy is aeroenergy, the extraphysical energy in the air. This energy is sometimes perceived visually in a spontaneous way, when we relax and look up, or when we look at the ocean, to the horizon.

Our objective in this technique is to see the aeroenergy and it is much easier to do this in an open space, where you can see the sky, preferably covering your field of vision completely. Look for a park or go to the beach or countryside and find a place where you can lie down, look up, and only see the sky. Ideally, you should not have buildings, trees, or lampposts, in your field of vision, only the sky.

Glasses can get in the way a little bit in this technique, since the edges of the lenses will be visible and the outer areas of your field of vision will be out of focus (if you are nearsighted). It will be better to wear contact lenses, if you have this option, as the borders will not be visible. If contact lenses are not an option you are better off with glasses than without, so at least you start with a sharp visual reference in the central portion of your field of vision.

The steps:

1. Start this technique with your eyes shut, and lying down in a comfortable position. In the first fifteen minutes, relax your body and your mind, and try to work with your energy body, particularly with the closed circuit of energies.

2. Next, try to blend your energies with the energies of nature around you. You should try this for about five minutes and try to absorb energies a bit, and try to feel and connect to the energy of the ground below your body.

3. Open your eyes and look at the sky. There is no need to set your vision on a particular spot at first. If you do this exercise on a clear day, the blue sky will not offer you any place to set your focal point to, a condition that often triggers clairvoyance on its own.

4. For at least five minutes, just keep your eyes open and try to stay receptive to any image you might detect.

5. Next, try to set your focal point to about ten meters above you, as if you were looking for a small object, or an insect

flying at that spot, a firefly for example. Continue as if you were trying to see the insect that someone told you is there, about ten meters away. You should spend at least ten minutes on this step, or until clairvoyance is triggered.

Aeroenergy is usually described as a series of bright white spots that move in a random fashion. The spots can cover part of your visual field, or all of it. The spots can appear to start from about two feet from you and continue for several meters. At times, you cannot see where this cloud of moving dots ends. The spots look "alive" and not like a passive source of light.

Those spots are the visual perception of the aeroenergy. Having abundant hydroenergy around, as is the case on the beach, or abundant geoenergy, as is the case in rocky mountains or earth chakras, seem to amplify this effect.

Outline Technique

You will need an assistant for this technique, sitting about six feet from you. Ideally, the background should be white, or at least of a uniform color. A bookshelf or busy desk with many objects on top can be distracting and could make it harder for you to detect the paravision input.

The technique can be applied while sitting or standing up. For deeper levels of relaxation, it would be best to have a recliner or comfortable sofa, one with the back high enough for you to rest your head on.

Illumination is important on this one, so make sure you observe the aspects described in the "Illumination" topic in the chapter "Optimizer Factors for Clairvoyance." Avoid natural light coming from the back of your assistant. If the background behind your assistant is a curtain and there is a window behind it, it will be best to apply this technique at night, unless you cover the window with something completely opaque, like cardboard or aluminum foil.

Your assistant should be between ten and fifteen feet from the wall, so that when your focal point is on the assistant, the wall is slightly out of focus.

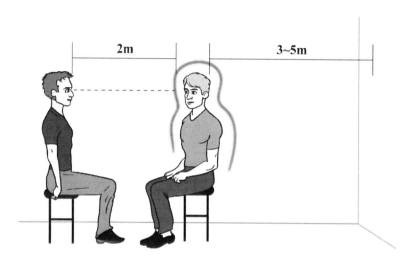

Figure 18: Outline Technique

The steps:

1. Close your eyes and relax your physical body. Look for mental serenity, stay lucid, and work with energies for ten minutes.

2. Open your eyes, focus on a spot in the air an inch from the arm of the assistant, and follow an imaginary line that is an inch away from the surface of the assistant's body. This line goes from halfway of the left upper arm to halfway on the right upper arm, going around the shoulders, neck, and head.

3. Move the focal point of your vision slowly so that it takes about three minutes to go from one side to the other.

4. Keep following the line and establish a slow cycle: when you reach the right arm move in the opposite direction, moving the focal point of your vision above the top of your assistant's head again, then reaching the starting point on

his left arm, where you initiate a new cycle.

You will be attempting to see the energosoma, the energy layer closest to the physical body, as you move your focal point. It is common to see the energosoma on the opposite side from where you are looking directly. In other words, as you follow the outline of the left shoulder you see energies above the right shoulder. You can stop moving your eyes for a moment if it happens, but stay focused on the left shoulder, and try to increase your relaxation to tune in to that perception, until you manage to see the entire bright outline around the assistant.

Dot in the Background Technique

You will also need an assistant for this one. You will be sitting face to face, two to three yards apart, and the assistant should be about 20 inches from the wall.

The wall should have a black dot with a diameter of three-quarter inch (two centimeters). Ideally, the black dot should be printed or drawn on paper with matte finish (not glossy). As most of us will not be willing to paint a black dot on the wall, a

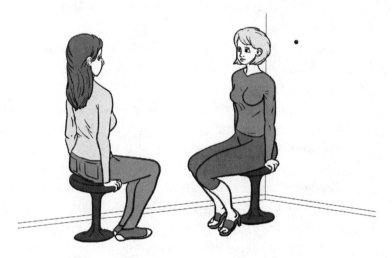

Figure 19: Dot in the Background Technique

simple solution is to cut a circle from black electric tape and attach it to the background wall.

Another possibility is to print a large dot on a white piece of paper, or draw one on white paper with a black marker, and attach it to the wall with mask tape.

The black spot should be at the height of your assistant's ear, and about four inches (ten centimeters) to the right from his left ear.

A low-light condition is preferred, ideally coming from an indirect source. A diffuse source of light, or multiple sources of dimmed light, would reduce shadows behind your assistant, which would be helpful for this technique.

The steps:

1. Close your eyes, relax your physical body, and try to be in a serene frame of mind. Stay lucid and work with your energies for ten minutes.

2. Open your eyes and look straight at the black dot on the wall. Keep the focal point of your vision and your attention on the black dot. Try not to look at the assistant directly.

3. After a few minutes try to use your peripheral vision to observe the energosoma of the assistant on the side of her body that is opposite to the black dot. You will keep the central part of your vision on the black dot. When you manage to see the energosoma, allow several seconds for you to get a stable tuning of this perception. After that you can continue your exploration and try to see other elements of the aura and extraphysical dimension.

The procedure above is simple and effective to see the energosoma, and a great way to start experimenting with clair-voyance.

Plant Energosoma Technique

You can apply this technique while lying under a healthy mature tree, positioned in such a way that you can see a branch, preferably a thicker one with more bioenergy, in the central part of your visual field.

It is important to find a comfortable position since this exercise lasts thirty minutes in total. If you lie down on the grass, it is better to use a towel, blanket, or mat to block the humidity. A mat can also help to create a more comfortable condition.

Look for a place in the shade and consider the sun movement when ensuring you will still be in the shade after 30 minutes.

Figure 20: Plant Energosoma Technique

The steps:

1. Start by finding a comfortable position, then relax and work with energies for ten or fifteen minutes.

2. Open your eyes and focus on a spot in the air, one inch from the tree branch, in a line starting between your eyes

and tangent to this branch. Try to tune into the energosoma of the tree.

3. Slow down your thoughts, and try to be tranquil. You should try to establish a connection with the tree by "thinking and feeling" like a tree, trying to imprint a pattern on your own energies that is closer to the consciousness-tree that you are looking at.

4. Aim at integrating your energies with the energies of the tree. Look for an energetic coupling based on relaxation, serenity, and openness of your own energies. Allow the temporary fusion between your field of energies and the field of energies of the tree. You should dedicate around ten minutes to this step. The energy connection will help with clairvoyance.

5. You can observe directly or try to use your peripheral vision, and alternate between trying to tune into seeing the energosoma of the tree and the outer portion of its field of energies. With time, you will be able to identify differences in clairvoyance perceptions between trees of different species, and even between trees of the same species.

A variation of this technique consists of sitting in a comfortable chair about twenty yards from the tree. You can use a camping chair, a chaise longue, or even a beach chair. Ideally, the chair should allow you to rest your head in a position where you can see the tree trunk with your eyes at rest, i.e., not looking up, down, or to the sides. The initial steps are the same, but in this case you will focus on a tangent point of the tree trunk, about an inch from the bark, trying to tune into the energetic body of the tree.

In a second variation the position does not matter as much: you can be lying down, sitting, or even standing, depending on the level of relaxation you need to trigger your paravision. In this variant you will look at the upper part of the tree, around the tree top. Find a large tree, preferably one that is very leafy, and on a sunny day, and position yourself where you can see the tree top with the blue sky as a background. The sun should be behind you, ideally, so that the excess light does not interfere with the observation. Try to tune into the aura of the tree right above the treetop.

Palmchakra Field Technique

A traditional technique consists of placing your hands parallel to one another, about five inches apart, and accumulating energies between them in order to detect non-physical energies on the palmcharkas or the field of energies that is formed in between. We will use this procedure, but try to see the field of energies and conduct a few experiments with our paravision.

We already know that densified energies are easier to see through clairvoyance. The slight accumulation of energies between your hands should help in that sense.

A reduced lighting condition will help, and you should pick a position that eliminates shadows of your arms on your lap or background surface.

The steps:

1. Start by sitting on a chair, with your eyes closed and placing your hands on your lap. Try to relax for five minutes.
2. After that, work with the closed circuit of energies for another five minutes. This will help you unblock, loosen, and activate your energosoma.
3. Place your hands parallel to each other and about four inches apart, with the palms facing each other, with your forearms a couple of inches above your legs, so that your hands will be at the same height as the belly button.
4. Still with your eyes closed, try to concentrate energies between your hands, by exteriorizing through both palm

chakras. Try to move and feel your energies flowing through your arms, reaching your hand, and slowly accumulating between your hands to create a small field of energies. It is not necessary to imagine or to visualize anything, you can simply use a mental command and focus on what you are trying to achieve. You may identify sensations as the energies accumulate, and have sensations of itching, tickling, "electricity," buzzing, and gentle touches on the tip of your fingers. Those can be energy sensations that indicate your will command to move energies is working.

5. After approximately five minutes concentrating energies between your hands, open your eyes and focus on an imaginary spot between your hands, as if a mosquito was exactly at that spot and you wanted to see this mosquito in detail.

You may have to adjust the position of your head in the beginning, as you look down. Try to make this adjustment right at the start and not to move your head anymore during the exercise.

Common perceptions in this technique are as follows: to see a small "cloud" between your hand, colors, spiral or circular movement, sparks, small spots of energy moving, a bright outline around your hands (your energosoma), background distortions as if the energy between your hands worked as a lens.

It is also possible that you perceive the air "change color" around your hands instead of seeing the palm chakra field, which usually means that you tuned into the energy of the umbilicochakra. The color is often green and the effect depends on how active you have this chakra during the exercise.

An optimization for this exercise is to use two large pieces of heavyweight paper, such as a poster board, in 11 x 17 inches or A3 size, one black and one white, preferably with matte finish, and have those on your lap as a background. You can start the exercise with the white background and, after about five minutes of observation, place the white sheet aside and work on the same exercise with a black background. You should try to move your physical body as little as possible during the exchange to maintain the relaxation level.

If you use this thick paper as a background, you can also set the focal point of your physical vision on the background, instead of between your hands. Reduced illumination and paper with a matte finish will make it hard to find the exact location of the surface of the paper, which is a good thing. The attempt to find the surface with the physical vision can trigger clairvoyance in such conditions.

A darker color works too if you cannot find a black poster board. The objective is to try clairvoyance with different backgrounds and to create a condition that helps you see colors in the energy that you might not have detected with the alternate background.

Some workshop participants preferred the white background, while others indicated a preference for the darker one. Most could detect differences in observation after changing the background. The exercise creates a great condition to observe nuances of your extraphysical perception, especially for those who only see a white fog in other exercises.

With the black background, it is a good idea to look for varia-tions of "texture" or "brightness" of the air in the area around half an inch from your physical body. Compare the perception you have of this layer with one background and the other.

You can also apply this technique with the lights on, especially with the white background. Bright white fluorescent lights, typically found in work environments, are particularly good to create a condition where it is easier to detect the energosoma around your hands.

This technique provides a good setup for you to try to

learn how to change clairvoyance tuning at will. You can use the 90/10 technique described in Chapter 4, "Clairvoyance Characteristics," under "Techniques to Change Clairvoyance Tuning." In summary, the 90/10 technique consists of dividing your attention and shifting a small part of it to your frontochakra. Energies will then tend to accumulate in the frontochakra and activate it. As an exercise, you can try to think about the point between your eyebrows while you read this words, and perhaps you will start to feel a gentle pressure in that area, or as if a feather was touching the base of your forehead in a very gentle manner.

There are other ways to work with your frontochakra while you have the field of energies between your hands. You can slowly exteriorize energies from your frontochakra and attempt to connect it to that energy field you created with your palmchakras. The maneuver can trigger clairvoyance, or change its tuning.

Dark Room Technique

The principle here is to create a condition where physical vision cannot work. We can achieve this by eliminating an essential element for its functioning: physical light. The idea is to create a completely dark environment, where it is physically impossible to see the physical dimension even with your eyes open.

When you have your eyes open in this environment, you will create an interesting condition: you expect and want to see something with your eyes, but you cannot. The combination of "want to see" and "cannot see" is important for this technique and, for this reason, the environment must be completely dark. Creating such environment is not as easy as it sounds, but the effort is worthwhile. Any source of light, even the faintest one, will allow you to see the outline of objects in the room after your eyes adjust to the dark, so we have to make sure that no source of light is present.

Another aspect we need to control during our experiment is the movement of our eyes and head, since movement can generate a variation in pressure inside the eyes and produce physical visual perceptions of diffuse color patches, shapes, and patterns, a phenomenon known as phosphenes.

It is not enough to simply switch off the lights and have "blackout" curtains to get complete darkness in a room. Any light, even an LED from an electronic device, street light from the outside reflected multiple times through the space between the wall and the curtain, or light coming through the space under the door are enough to interfere with the process.

As a general rule, it is easier to apply this technique at night and therefore eliminating a very powerful light source: the sun. A room without windows or with a small window can be helpful. The best way to cover a window is with aluminum foil. You can make aluminum foil stick to glass by wetting the glass with a bit of water and detergent, and making sure that the aluminum foil covers the edges, all the way to the window frame.

Covering a window with paper or curtains is usually not enough since those materials let a bit of light through. Most types of blackout curtains and even cardboard will usually let some light through the edges. It usually takes at least 20 minutes for your eyes to adjust and for you to start to see the light "leaks." To prevent light coming through a door you can hang a thick blanket from the outside.

You will know that you have a completely dark room if you cannot see the outlines of objects in the room, even after twenty minutes. Seeing shapes from physical objects or physical features of the room means that there is light coming from somewhere.

It is necessary to allow ample time for your physical eyes to adjust to the lighting condition. Our eyes depend on specific cells to see in darker conditions, different from those we use in bright conditions. When you switch off the lights, a slow biochemical process begins, and it takes dozens of minutes for the cells that work in low light conditions to be ready. If you see bright light again, you will saturate those cells again, and need time to allow them to be ready to send images to your brain.

To avoid tripping or bumping into something in the dark it would be a good idea to have an LED flashlight with you, like one of those that are sold as key chains. Red light tends to saturate your low-light retina cells at a slower pace, so a red LED would be ideal. Having this source of light is helpful to get to and from the chair you will use in the experiment. For obvious reasons, it is not recommended that you move around the room when it is completely dark.

The technique starts, therefore, after at least twenty minutes in the dark room, time you can use to work with your energies and relax. You should be sitting in a chair to avoid going to sleep, but could try this while lying down in bed if you have difficulties with relaxation and falling asleep is not a problem.

After the time to allow your eyes to adjust and with your eyes open, make sure you are unable to see anything while having your head and eyes still. You can move your head side to side to experience the phosphene phenomenon, which will help you differentiate this physical perception from clairvoyance perceptions later on. You can also to move your eyes from side to side without moving your head to detect a more subtle phosphene phenomenon.

After this initial procedure, make sure that you keep your head and your eyes steady as you try the experiments below.

Experiment: Palmchakra

Take your right hand close to your right eye, with the palm facing your eye, and see if you can detect the energy interaction between your hand and your energy body. You can try a gentle exteriorization through the palm chakra and try to detect this exteriorization visually. Accumulating energies in your hand or exteriorizing through your hand can also generate interesting visual *para*perceptions. Moving your hand can be interesting too, but in this case it would be a bit harder to be certain that the movement did not cause the phosphene effect.

Experiment: Arm Energosma

Rest one of your arms on a surface next to you and position yourself so that the arm is in the central area of your visual field. You can use a desk or other piece of furniture to rest your arm, and should find a comfortable position where you can observe your forearm looking straight at it. Lifting your arm or resting it in your lap would not work, as you would have to apply effort to keep the arm in front of you or tilt your head to see your forearm.

Once you establish a comfortable position, take about five minutes examining the area where your arm is. Since you are in complete darkness you should not see anything at first, although you would know that you that your arm is there. The objective is to detect differences in brightness, "texture," or color between the area where your arm is and the surrounding areas. You can also try to detect the edge of your arms, or the shape of your energosoma. Another experiment is to detect the effect of concentrating energies in your forearm or exteriorizing energies through it.

Experiment: Frontochakra Exteriorization

With your head straight, aligned with your spine, and looking forward, start to exteriorize pulses of energies through your frontochakra. You can alternate and wait a few seconds between gathering energies around this chakra and exteriorizing. When you exteriorize, try to reach forward with your energies for three to four feet.

Try to intensify the exteriorization, stay relaxed, and not to move your head. As you exteriorize, try to see the interaction of the energies with the surroundings as you do it. You may see colors changing as you exteriorize, a common perception with this experiment.

Experiment: Observe the Energosoma of a Plant

If it is possible to place a plant in the room you prepared for the experiment, you can try to see its energosoma and the interactions between your energy and the energy of the plant.

A lush and leafy plant tends to have more energies, and therefore an energosoma that is easier to detect. Some workshop participants suggested that watering the plant before the experiment made the energies more visible. Others indicated that the energosoma of plants that were outside the house before the experiment showed more energies than those always indoors.

Experiment: See the Aura of an Assistant

This will require an assistant with a bit more willingness to help, or perhaps someone close that is also interested in clairvoyance.

Once both have adjusted the physical vision to the dark condition, the first activity can consist of trying to see each other's aura. You can also request the assistant to exteriorize energies and try to detect the exteriorization with your paravision.

The assistant can also decide when to exteriorize at random, allowing you to verify if your visual paraperceptions matched his action after the experiment. The assistant could tap his foot, for example, and decide to exteriorize or not after doing so. He could, after the experiment, share if an exteriorization happened or not. After a few attempts you could check your perceptions with the assistant, and train towards increasing the number of times you make a correct identification.

Semispheres Technique

Several experiments of extraphysical perception (or extrasensory perception) use two white semispheres placed over the subject's eyes, with the concave side facing inwards, towards the eyes, in order to give a constant, random stimulus to physical vision.

The cheapest version of this setup is to use a white ping-pong ball split in half. A more comfortable version consists of painting the inside of a swimming goggles with white correction fluid, letting the fluid accumulate on the corners a bit so those corners are rounded off once the fluid dries up.

It will be impossible to see with a white surface so close to your eyes since that would require a short focal point that is not reachable with the lens we have inside our eyes. The light reaching your eyes will be diffuse, since the surface of the ping-pong ball, or the dry correction fluid will have a matte finish. With time, the sensation will be that you are looking at a very dense fog.

This sensation of looking at something "endless" is essential for this technique, and it is similar to the "Dark Room Technique" in the sense that you keep your eyes open and want to see something without being physically able to do so. Additionally, you will be unable to set your physical vision in a place within focal distance, where you would see a sharp image. Both conditions can help you find the "switch" that start clairvoyance.

Personally, I prefer the dark room technique because there is no physical barrier in front of my eyes (i.e., the semispheres). A personal paradigm might be at play here, since we are familiar with the fact that covering your eyes interrupts vision, while we rarely find ourselves in room with absolutely no light.

Many people, however, find the semispheres technique more practical and obtain good results with it. You do not need a lot of preparation work for this technique, so it is worth a try.

You can do this technique while sitting down, but the ideal would be to lie down, or at least to sit in a reclining chair, to allow for a deeper relaxation. A bit of light or a fully lit room work well for this experiment and will more easily produce the "thick fog" effect earlier described.

Start with your eyes shut, then relax and work with energies for about 15 minutes. After that you can open your eyes and try to detect changes in color in front of you. Physical vision allows you to see white only in this condition, so any color perception is an indication that your paravision started to work.

The palmchakra experiment explained in the Dark Room Technique and exteriorizing through your frontochakra can also be used in conjunction with the semispheres technique.

Facial Clairvoyance Technique

I learned this technique in a class at the IIPC – International Institute of Projectiology and Conscientiology – in Curitiba, Brazil, and have practiced and taught this technique for many years. This technique is also used in a laboratory called Acoplamentarium, at CEAEC, the Center for Higher Studies of Consciousness, in Iguaçu Falls, Brazil.

The technique consists of looking at the face of another person in front of you, an intraphysical consciousness, at a distance between six and thirty feet, in a room with dimmed lights, with indirect illumination.

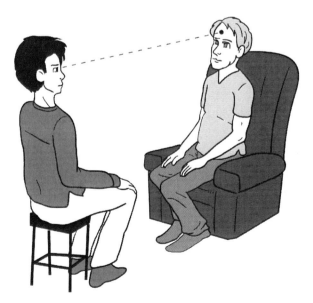

Figure 21: Facial Clairvoyance

This technique is done with participants sitting down and obser-vation time can last up to twenty minutes.

For this exercise, the ideal is to find an experimenter that you trust and have affinity with, preferably someone with a more objective approach, less mystical, without major intrusion and a higher cosmoethical standard (see topic "Deassimilation and Discernment" in Chapter 6).

Make sure that you can see the face of the other participant before starting this technique. If necessary, adjust your position or illumination, and make sure you can see him directly in front of you, without obstructions.

Try to minimize visual stimuli on the background behind the person you are looking at by removing colorful objects, moving objects, books, paintings, and so on. The ideal background here would be a wall painted in white or a light color.

The steps:
1. Start with your eyes closed, sitting with your back straight. Work with energies for ten or fifteen minutes, applying the closed circuit of energies and trying to reach the vibra-tional state. Then exteriorize energies to help densify the field around you and the other experimenter.
2. Open your eyes and look at the tip of the nose of the other participant. What is important here is to stay focused on a single spot for a prolonged period of time. You can pick another spot to look at, such as the top of his forehead, tip of the right ear, or a spot that is an inch before the tip of his nose. Some people prefer to look at the highest point on the other person's head, leaving that person's face outside the central area of physical vision, something that can facilitate clairvoyance. Once you make a choice, do not change it for at least five minutes. This exercise demands persistence and changing the focal point too often will reduce its effec-tiveness significantly.

3. Stay serene while you observe the face of the other person and the surroundings. The most common impediment in this exercise is anxiety. The observation with your eyes open should take between ten and twenty minutes.

4. Openness in energetic terms also helps. Ideally, you should allow or promote an energetic coupling during this exercise.

5. Pay attention to changes in the face, in the aura of the other participant, and in the energies in the surrounding areas. Try to perceive the presence of extraphysical consciousnesses in the room during the experiment and make mental notes of everything.

6. To finalize the exercise, close your eyes and work on a closed circuit of energies. Take advantage of your condition of relaxation to better perceive the energies as you move them up and down. The main objective of this essential last step is to break the energetic coupling with the other participant(s), both intraphysical and extraphysical, which normally happens during the exercise. The energetic *de*coupling concludes the exercise, ensuring that you don't carry any energy remnants with you. It is also good to reach a vibrational state at the end of the exercise, as it will increase your energetic homeostasis.

The facial clairvoyance technique allows you to see the extraphysical dimension indirectly. You will be able to see the face of an *extraphysical* consciousness over the face of an *intraphysical* consciousness you are looking at.

It is common to have the impression that the height or width of the room you are in has changed during the exercise. The effect seems to happen when you start to mix the physical visual input with the extraphysical visual input. Perceived variation of illumination is also common, even when the physical illumination does not change at all during the exercise.

The accounts below, from different people in different exercises, are typical of this kind of technique:

Account 1:

When I opened my eyes I had the sensation that I was inside of a cloud, all I could see was white... There was a type of fog in the room that, in some moments, was so dense that you [the instructor] would disappear completely...

Account 2:

Your face was completely dark at a point, as if someone placed a hood over your head. At some point, later, I saw a face emerge from this dark area; it was a face different from yours, from a young Chinese woman, perhaps twenty years old, a delicate complexion, but a very stern way of looking... She was a very serious young lady.

Account 3:

First, I saw everything around me with a type of electricity. It looked as if all the furniture and people had this very interesting "vibrating brightness." Next, I started to see everything as in the negative film, your white shirt became black, and your darker pants looked silver-white. Then I saw a man with a beard, but a man with shoulders a lot wider, and a taller man. I see now [after the exercise] the difference compared to your [the instructor] body. The man looked like a longshoreman, or a sailor, something along those lines, very strong, the appearance or the energy transmitted this idea. I could also see your [the instructor's] coronochakra, as a disc towards the back of your head, and some waves of energy from about two feet on your left.

Account 4:

I saw several faces, five more or less, all with black skin. The majority were men, perhaps one was a woman, or had a more feminine face. The majority had a neutral expression, and one, in particular, had a kind of sad expression. Now, I saw all of them with a lot of detail, I even moved my head and blinked at some point and the face was still there, it was really impressive.

Account 5:

The face I have seen more clearly was like an Indian woman, with very dark and long hair, and darker skin.

[Instructor]: Native American Indian?

No, the face and clothing was closer to a pre-Hispanic Mexican. Long straight hair.

[Instructor]: Did you perceive her pattern of energies?

Yes, it was a very tranquil pattern. She was looking directly at me, as if you turned your face to me [turning about 30 degrees]. She transmitted a very strong energy. I think I have seen her before in an out-of-body experience.

The age, origin, ethnicity, and period in history that can be inferred by the clothing, jewelry, hairstyle, and facial hair, can also vary a lot. It is a good idea to study the basics of those aspects to describe your perceptions better. You can learn, for example, how to recognize when a hat belongs to the late nineteenth century in Europe or when facial features suggest a particular ethnicity. This can lead to more detailed perceptions and better rapport with the consciousness that you are seeing. It will also provide more information for you and help in the inter-pretation of the parapsychic event.

One theory to explain facial clairvoyance is that the energosoma close to our face is denser and can be molded by the extraphysical consciousness as she connects or make contact with the energosphere of the person you are looking at.

There are cases – less frequent ones – where the face seen during facial clairvoyance represents a past life of the person you are looking at, or even a face you had in a past life. Although those are possibilities, I can say based on experience that the face identified is from an extraphysical consciousness that is present in the room, at least 95 percent of the time.

Conscientiological theory indicates that a past life recall comes with a strong energetic impact and with further information about that past life. A past life recall is impactful to the extent that you recognize a very specific energetic "signature" from one of your past lives, making it very different from imagination, dreaming, or a perception that is casually noticed. Another rule of thumb is that a past life recall is backed by characteristics of the experimenter in the current life: key skills, mannerisms, and traits can take a long time to change, and should be in line of the overall picture from the prior life.

Waldo Vieira indicates other possible outcomes of this exercise in the treatise Projectiology, though more rare ones, such as seeing scenery from a place nearby.

An extraphysical consciousness could, technically, mold any face as a thought-form, using energies from the person that we are looking at, although this is another very rare possible outcome. In order to identify this type of event you can try to connect energetically with the face you are seeing. A thought form will feel "inert," devoid of life, like looking at the face of a wax figure in a museum. Connecting with an extraphysical consciousness is very different, and you will feel the specific pattern of thought and energy of that conscex, which is often strikingly different from the pattern of the intraphysical consciousness that is facilitating the phenomenon.

The quality of energy and facial expression of the extraphysical consciousness can change a lot, and depend on which one you tune in during the exercise.

Facial clairvoyance exercises produce positive experiences in the vast majority of cases, especially when the participants manage the holothosene established with discernment, and when energy work is adequately applied. Experimenters often see consciousnesses that transmit serenity and security and, at the same time, trigger an intuition that they are there to help. There are also countless accounts of visual perception of energies of incredible beauty and with very interesting characteristics, some so different from physical visual perception that make it hard to describe it in physical terms.

Sequence of Different Faces

The face you see during a facial clairvoyance exercise can change very quickly and show dozens of faces in a less than a minute. The account below illustrates this relatively common phenomenon:

> I saw a series of faces that appeared very quickly [over the instructor's face], as if it was a slideshow, with each face remaining a short amount of time. The faces were of men, women, young and old… Very interesting…
>
> [Instructor]: Any particular one stay for a longer period? Anyone call your attention?
>
> […] The faces changes very quickly, and there were lots of them. This constant change lasted three, maybe five minutes… I saw a fog after that, a white light in your face, then after that there was one face that I could see in more detail.

Accounts like the one above are common, and some react with surprise when experiencing it for the first time. It seems that the experience helps with a specific element in the multidimensional awareness of the experimenter, conveying a simple yet powerful message, something that seems to connect the person to the wider multidimensional community we live in.

In a typical exercise this fast sequence of faces can happen with up to ten percent of the participants. The frequency of change is typically one face per second but can reach a few faces per second. At times, the changes are so quick that the experimenter can barely discern the details of each particular face.

One theory for this quick change is based on the concept of clairvoyance tuning, explained earlier. In an environment full of extraphysical people, some will reach a specific altered state of consciousness where they can "sweep" across many "channels," each one associated with the specific holothosene of one of the consciousnesses in the room.

The Globe Technique

While trying the facial-clairvoyance technique, you may get stuck in specific dimensional tuning of clairvoyance that does not let you see faces. For example, you may see a dense fog in front of you, or a sort of thick smoke in front of the person you are observing, but no changes in faces for the remainder of the exercise.

To change the clairvoyance tuning in those cases you can apply the Globe Technique. The procedure consists of trying to find the outer edge of the first layer of the aura in an area above the forehead, on the front side of the person. This area would be more or less five inches from the top of the forehead, on a straight line going upwards at a forty-five-degree angle.

To spot that area of the aura, you need to scan the area by changing the focal point of your physical vision up, down, and back and forth, until you change the positional tuning of your clairvoyance and start to see the spherical shape of the surface of the first layer of the aura. After clairvoyance sets in, you can see about two thirds of a sphere around the head of the person, as if that person's head was in inside a globe.

Just trying to find the outer edge of the first layer of the aura may be enough to trigger facial clairvoyance. If that does not happen, you can follow the imaginary line we described earlier with your physical sight. This line is on a forty-five-degree angle, going upward, and you should follow it from the spot five inches away from the top of the forehead to the top of the forehead of the person you are observing. You should attempt this only after you identify the aura of the person on the far side of the line. As you concentrate on following the line, the faces may start to show, or you might be able to tune into different faces.

Dimmed Lights and Implicit Suggestion

A frequent question related to this technique is as follows: Could it be that the faces we see in this exercise are from our imagination, triggered by the low lighting condition of the room?

Accounts containing the segments similar to the ones below seem to invite this question:

I could see your face, but you were sporting a beard.

I could see your face, but about ten years older.

I continued to see the face of the instructor, but he looked younger.

Although the comments above could be derived from *extraphysical* perceptions, they are more often than not an interpretation of *intraphysical* perception, temporarily limited due to the dimmed conditions.

A way to clear any doubts and solve this dilemma is to go deeper in the perception. The goal should be to see the face clearly, to get to the point where the perception "locks in," and will not go away even if you move your head a bit or blink. For that, you need to stay cool, and allow the phenomenon to develop, and wait a bit longer.

One analogy that I use in classes is to say that when the face begins to appear, you should have the mental attitude of "leaning back" instead of "leaning forward." It is along the lines of thinking, "Yes, I can see something, I am interested, but I am not impressed at this point. I want to see more, but I am not in a hurry."

You can also repeat the experiment several times to try to

reach a point where you see an extraphysical face that is completely different from the face of the intraphysical person you are looking at. For example, if the intraphysical person you are looking at has very masculine facial features, and has blond hair and instead, during the exercise, you see a Chinese woman with very feminine and delicate facial features, who has black hair. With a perception like this, it is easier to say that its origin was was extraphysical and not something derived from suggestion or association of ideas.

Effect of Exteriorization of Energies

A recommendation for facial clairvoyance experiments is to exteriorize energies before the facial clairvoyance attempt in order to create better conditions for visual paraperceptions.

Field experience shows that exteriorizing *while* attempting facial clairvoyance often interferes with this particular exercise, causing the faces to "disappear" or to change very quickly..

Mirror and Impressionability

A mirror is something simple from the intraphysical point of view: a surface that reflects light, allowing us to see something outside our normal line of sight. A mirror is not positive or negative, good or bad. It is an object that reflects images. Our subjective experience with it, however, might not be that simple.

Personal experience as well as countless accounts indicate that a mirror can also, somehow, "reflect" extraphysical images, from the energetic dimension and from the extraphysical dimension. Although some hypotheses exist to explain this phenomenon, the mechanism through which an aura is reflected in the mirror, for example, is not known at this point.

The reason to approach this subject is the frequently asked question: can I do a clairvoyance exercise in the mirror? The short answer is – it depends.

If we analyze the references to the mirror in the last five

centuries, from a cultural standpoint, we will find several mystical and magical connotations associated with this type of object. Breaking a mirror brings seven years of bad luck; mirrors do not reflect the image of a vampire; the queen in the Snow White story would talk to an entity that lived inside of the mirror, and so on.

Several movies produced in recent decades contain situations where someone sees ghosts, spirits, fairies, and demons reflected in a mirror. The majority of those movies are in the horror, thriller, or suspense categories. The mirror, therefore, ends up associated symbolically, in popular terms, with a world "beyond" this one, or to the extraphysical dimension, but in a negative way.

Due to the commercial exploitation of horror movies, a popular genre among teenagers, the mirror can have an even more negative connotation, especially when one is in a room with low lighting conditions. The experimenter can feel a bit uneasy or fearful in front of the mirror, even without realizing it at first, as those emotions can be rooted in subconscious parts of the mind.

Given this context, I usually don't recommend clairvoyance exercises with a mirror, at least not to the general public. For an experimenter with self-confidence and good practice with deassimilation and energy work, however, working with a mirror would not be an issue.

We can use an analogy to understand this recommendation. I would not consider it to be intelligent to see open-heart surgery "just for fun." The images of the heart beating, the surgeon cutting through skin and bone, and all the blood involved, can be impactful and even traumatizing for a person that is not prepared. A young individual planning to get into medical school could even give up the career if the experience happened without preparation or at the wrong time.

On the other hand, if that individual had studied a bit of

anatomy and cultivated a sense of relaxed and bold curiosity towards natural aspects of our physical body, the same experience could be very educational.

Clairvoyance exercises in the mirror can be compared to this context. There is nothing "unnatural" or unbearably ugly about what you can see. However, the experience can have a negative impact on some, depending on the context and extraphysical environment of the individual, and could perhaps demotivate the experimenter in his parapsychic development.

If you work with someone else in clairvoyance exercises the symbolism and mystery of the mirror is out of the equation.

An experimenter that prepares the extraphysical environment through an exteriorization of energies, creating a positive environment, and uses the closed circuit of energies to reach a vibrational state, before and after the exercise, and stays confident and serene while applying the technique, can achieve productive and interesting results with or without the mirror. I have heard a considerable amount of accounts reporting positive experiences with a mirror.

A criterion that you can use to gauge your level of self-confidence and assess if working with a mirror is for you, at the point you are currently at is as follows: if you do not feel a hundred percent comfortable sitting in a dark room for at least 20 minutes with your eyes open, while alone in your house, then the mirror is not for you. You are better off working with other exercises until you feel at ease in this reference condition.

We know that the pattern of our thoughts and sentiments evokes – or calls with energy – consciousnesses with a similar pattern. If your pattern is along the lines of "I am here to learn and help in whatever possible, and I am aiming for a higher level of cosmoethics and understanding of things," the tendency is to attract and be supported by helpers. A holothosene that is serene, focused on helping others (assistantial), and with a healthy curiosity, is associated with positive and enriching clairvoyance experiences.

Concentration Technique

Waldo Vieira presents this technique as a procedure to produce out-of-body experiences. The reason why I describe this technique in this chapter is because it has helped me with clairvoyance development. I had several clairvoyance perceptions every time I applied the concentration technique, from simply seeing the energetic dimension, to more elaborate instances where I could see extraphysical beings in the same room.

The exercise consists of looking at the flame of a short candle placed on top of a large ceramic plate and about ten feet away. You should be sitting on a comfortable sofa or recliner, preferably with your head resting on a pillow. Your head should be positioned so that you see the candle in front of you without straining your eyes looking up or down, and in a position that allows you to relax the neck and shoulder muscles.

As a safety measure, you should use a short candle, cut down to one or two inches long, and use the molten wax to fixate it to the ceramic plate underneath it. A regular ceramic dining plate, about eight inches in diameter, would work well, so the flame would be contained even if the candle fell to the side during the experiment.

It is also important to make sure that nothing can fall on top of the flame, like a curtain or piece of clothing, and cause a fire. You can place the flame inside a large transparent jar made of glass with the opening facing upwards. If you are uneasy, in doubt, or only have a small room available, use a flameless battery-based candle simulator, something you can find in party stores.

If you use a real candle, the geometry of the candle matters. Ideally, you should use a solid candle, without hollow channels parallel to the wick. The molten wax flowing in a messy and random way will make the flame unstable, which is good to keep your attention for a longer period of time. The diameter of the candle should be less than an inch. Thicker candles tend to generate a short flame that does not move as much. A thin birthday candle can work, as long as it burns for long enough and allows you enough time to apply the clairvoyance technique.

The wick construction matters as well: the combination of wick and wax composition determines the height of the flame. A wick with too few threads tends to produce a weak flame. The goal is to have a long and dynamic flame, one that is easy for the experimenter to concentrate on.

The steps:
1. Start the exercise with a ten-minute closed circuit of energies, aiming at installing the vibrational state.
2. Open your eyes and focus directly on the flame. Focus exclusively on the flame and in its movements. The projective technique is a bit more elaborate from this point forward, however, for clairvoyance purposes it is enough to look at the flame and forget the world around you.
3. Keep your eyes open, avoid moving your physical body and silence your thoughts. Concentrate exclusively on the flame for at least twenty minutes. The perceptions described in the section "Beginning of Extraphysical Perception" in Chapter 4 are very common in this technique.
4. To finalize the technique, close your eyes and work with a closed circuit of energies once more, trying to reach the vibrational state.

There are several aspects that facilitate clairvoyance in the procedure above. Dimmed lights help to reduce the physical visual stimulus and make it easier to detect the paravision stimulus.

Another aspect is that you will have something very bright in the central portion of your vision, the flame, in sharp contrast against the penumbra on the surroundings and background. This condition will "disable" the central vision and force you to process the input from the outer areas of your field of region, a temporary imbalance that may trigger clairvoyance.

Additionally, there is something special about the variable brightness and random movement of the flame that makes it easy to concentrate on it for a longer period of time. You will be able to reach deeper levels of relaxation with a reasonable level of lucidity in the process, placing you in an optimized condition to access your parapsychic ability.

Hand Energosoma Technique

One of the characteristics of physical vision is its relatively slow response time, i.e., the relatively long time it takes for the image we perceive to change after an object has moved in front of us. This technique is built around this characteristic of our physical vision.

The slow retinal response is what makes the blades of a moving fan look like a blurry disk. The effect also contributes for movement in a video to appear continuous despite being a series of still frames being presented in quick succession.

Retinal persistence is not, of course, clairvoyance. What we will try to do is to trigger clairvoyance by observing "ghost" images produced by the retinal persistence effect. Observing those ghost images will help you explore visual sensations and change your focal point during an experiment. This activity will help you find the "switch" of your paravision.

As we propose using those ghost images as a stepping-stone, you may ask, how are we going to know what is a ghost image and what is actually clairvoyance during the exercise? The good news is that ghost images only happen if you "imprint" a certain pattern in your retina and then move your eyes. Ghost images fade quickly, in seconds, typically, and definitely within a minute, while clairvoyance tends to get clearer with time and to present steady brightness. The best way to learn to differentiate the two is to pay attention to *how* the ghost images fade. If you pay attention to this aspect alone, you will be able to identify clearly when the image is or is not derived from the retinal persistence effect.

The effects of retinal persistence are relatively easy to detect and describe, and a good way to establish language for subjective visual phenomena. For this reason, we will explore several techniques related to retinal persistence in this chapter.

The first technique involves observing your hands in a continuous movement. The goal is to detect the physical ghost images produced by retinal persistence, then observe your own energy body when your clairvoyance is triggered. You can apply this technique while sitting on a chair. You need a white cardboard sheet, sized 11 by 17 inches or bigger, sitting on your lap.

White light is ideal for this technique, preferably fluorescent light. The more contrast between your hand and the background the better.

The steps:

1. Place your hands in a fist, but with your index fingers extended and pointing to one another, as in the figure below.

2. Move your index fingers as close as possible to one another, but without touching, and start to pull them apart, following a horizontal straight line. It is important to try to keep your index fingers aligned with this straight imaginary line. Look at a spot on the background, on the paper, around the central point between your index fingers. Keep looking at this spot throughout the exercise.

3. When your index fingers are about four inches apart,

reverse the direction of movement and start bringing the tips of your index fingers closer. Move your hands slowly and make sure that your index fingers follow the horizontal line described earlier.

4. Start a cycle of moving the tip of your index fingers away and closer, and repeat this cycle fifteen times. Each cycle should take about one second. Avoid moving your head or your eyes. You will notice a faint bright trail along the horizontal line after a few cycles. Focus your vision on this trail for the remainder of the technique.

5. After repeating the cycle fifteen times, bring your index fingers very close to one another, but not touching, and start to pull your hands apart, but very slowly this time. It should take about ten seconds for you to reach the point when they are four inches apart.

Figure 22: Hand Energosoma Technique

As we indicated earlier, the logic behind this procedure is to use a physical ghost perception to trigger the visual *para*perception.

In the fifteen-cycle phase, with the rapid movement of your hands, the image persistence effect will generate a bright trail along the horizontal line followed by your index fingers. In the slow movement phase, you will give ample time for your eyes to adjust and eliminate the physical effect. By trying to "lock in" to the ghost image, you may trigger your clairvoyance. A bright, non-fading outline may appear around your hands at some point, indicating that you tuned in to the energetic dimension and were able to see the energosoma around your hands.

Another frequent perception is some sort of energy connection between the index fingers, but with brightness and thickness significantly different from the fading ghost image. Several reported the appearance of elasticity in this connection, as in rubber or chewing gum, when they pulled their hands apart. Sparks, white spots, blue and yellow hues around the hands were also reported frequently.

Chin-Forehead Technique
This is a variation of the previous technique that can be applied during a facial clairvoyance exercise.

The steps:
1. With a person sitting in front of you, about three feet away, look at the chin of this person and count to thirty. It is important not to move your head or your eyes during those thirty seconds to ensure that your retinas are receiving the image in the same physical area. You can count to thirty slowly if you like, precision in the amount of time is not important. Blinking is okay.
2. After those thirty seconds, look at the top of the forehead of the other person. Move your eyes only, and move them at once. A ghost image in the shape of the other person's head should appear above her head. This image fades quickly, in a few seconds usually, remaining a few dozen seconds at the most.
3. When you see the ghost image, look directly at the center of it and lock your attention on it as it fades. The tendency

is for the ghost image to fade and then you start seeing the aura of the other person, usually briefly at first, then for longer periods as you practice the exercise a few times.

Tips: the more contrast between the person you are looking at and the background, the better. You might want to try variations with more light or less light to amplify the effect. Try with the lights on at least once, and then try with dimmed lights, then on a darker setting. You can also increase the time to one minute to give your retina more time to "imprint" the ghost image.

Change of Lights Technique

This technique is also based on retinal image persistence effect, but relies on a quick change of lighting conditions and requires the participation of an assistant.

You and your assistant should be sitting about ten feet apart, facing each other. The background behind your assistant should be uniform, and not busy, ideally a plain wall painted white or a light color.

Two sources of light are needed: one direct and bright, one indirect and dimmed. In workshops, I would often rely on fluorescent lights at the ceiling, making sure that no shadows are seen on the background, and one of those hallway lights that can be plugged in the wall socket, with five watt of power or less, placed outside the field of vision of all participants.

The steps:

1. With both sources of light switched on and your eyes closed, start your relaxation process and work with your energies for ten minutes.
2. Open your eyes and look at the top of the forehead or to one of the shoulders of your assistant. Keeping your head and your eyes still is essential for this technique to work. Keep looking at the spot you have selected for one minute,

without moving your physical body. Your assistant should count the time.

3. The assistant switches off the strong and direct lights, leaving the weak indirect light as the only source in the room. The assistant should move as little as possible to switch off the lights. This means that the switch for the strong light should be very close, in a way that a slight movement of his arm can switch it off. If you have the bright light operated by remote control, or a third person that can count the time and switch off the lights, even better.

4. Due to the quick change in illumination conditions, you will not be able to see in the first couple of seconds or so. As your eyes start to adjust, you will see a bright outline around the assistant, an effect of the physical adjustment of your physical vision. Focus your physical vision on this bright outline and stay focused on this perception. The bright contour of physical origin will fade quickly and the transition should trigger your clairvoyance. When that happens, a thicker, brighter, and stable outline will be visible through clairvoyance. Other visual paraperceptions can follow as well depending on the tuning of your paravision.

In the conditions explained above your eyes should adjust in about thirty seconds. If you see sparks, flashes, bright contours, or similar visual perceptions after this time, then the source will not be your physical eyes. This exercise is helpful to examine the difference between the visualization of the energosoma through clairvoyance and the fading outline that has a physical origin. The energosoma is often described as having "life" and "texture," for example.

This technique is very effective for those who have never seen anything extraphysical, and helps with the accumulation of personal evidence of parapsychic phenomena.

Windshield Wiper Technique

While ghost images are helpful to trigger clairvoyance, especially in the beginning of your experiments, those can be a bit distracting on long-duration facial clairvoyance exercises, especially when performing experiments in lower lighting conditions. So I thought I should include a way to "cancel" image persistence during an experiment in case you find the need for it.

The technique is simple: it consists of moving your eyes side to side, by looking at a point about one foot away from the left cheek of the face of the other person, on a horizontal line, then about one foot from the right cheek. Alternate looking at those imaginary points, going back and forth at least three times, as if you were following a windshield wiper in front of you. Moving your eyes back and forth should take a bit over a second each time. This would be fast enough to even out the image imprint on your retina, making any ghost images go away.

I have used this as a "reset button" in many techniques, so I would go back to looking at a clear physical image only, then while at a deeper relaxation state, I would proceed to applying another technique.

One effect I noticed was that right after this "reset," if I managed to stay still and looking steadily at the face of the other person, I would start seeing his energies spontaneously.

Chapter 9

Clairvoyance and Other Phenomena

We will explore a few psychic phenomena in this chapter, particularly those that involve perception of images, and draw comparisons with clairvoyance. The main objective is to broaden the understanding of clairvoyance and its mechanisms, in order to facilitate the classification of experiences.

Some phenomena we will discuss can happen simultaneously with clairvoyance, or involve more variables than what is presented here. The approach adopted, however, is to present a "clear-cut" definition of each phenomenon, and to offer a clear reference that covers the majority of the cases.

Clear reference will help you classify and better understand your experiences, and those you hear about. With time and practice in analyzing the results of parapsychic exercises, it is likely that you will see nuance and complexity beyond the initial descriptions we will present.

Local Clairvoyance and Out-of-Body Experience (OBE)

The fundamental difference between both phenomena is that the psychosoma of the experimenter is *inside* the physical body during local clairvoyance. In an OBE, the psychosoma and the consciousness are both *outside* the physical body.

One of the ways to identify this difference is by examining the point of observation during the experience. Clear evidence of an OBE is when you see your own physical body from a point of view that is several feet away from it. An example of this type of event, involving OBE, is sometimes reported by people under full anesthesia, while in surgery. The patient reports seeing his own body from an observation point close to the ceiling. Accounts like this often include details of the operating theatre and actions from the medical team.

In contrast to this experience, if the patient was lying in bed and started to see the aura of a nurse, with his eyes open and from the natural perspective of his own body, we would then classify this phenomenon as clairvoyance.

Remote Viewing and Out-of-Body Experience

A bit more experience is required to tell these phenomena apart. The difference is technically simple: the psychosoma is completely *outside* of the physical body during an OBE, while almost completely *inside* the physical body during remote viewing.

Another difference is that the experimenter does not have control of the physical body in an OBE – except for the very rare instances of OBEs with the physical body in movement that typically have very short duration, measured in fractions of a second. In remote viewing, on the other hand, the experimenter can describe or make a drawing of the scenes observed from a distance while the phenomenon is happening.

Although OBE and Remote Viewing are fundamentally different, the only way to tell the difference in some cases is to evaluate if you "felt you were there" during the experience. This is a subjective evaluation, of course, and its accuracy is tied directly to the accumulation of experiences.

In fact, you would have no doubt that you out of the physical body in a lucid OBE. What I mean by lucidity is "how awake" you are in the experience. It is typically harder to classify experiences when the level of lucidity is lower, or when the experimenter does not have a good collection of experiences with varying levels of lucidity to compare and contrast.

One way of establishing the difference is to pay attention to how wide the angle of observation is during the experience. In an OBE, the observation angle tends to be the same or wider than the physical vision, in other words, a bit less than 180 degrees from left to right.

During remote viewing, the field of vision can be restricted at times, as if you were looking through a round opening, allowing your field to have 90 degrees of opening or less. It can feel like being inside a dark room and seeing through a hole on the wall.

Of course, not *all* remote viewing experiences have restricted field of vision. It is also hard to say for sure that not a single instance of OBE can have a restricted observation field. This variable should be used to give support (or not) to the hypothesis of one phenomenon or another while interpreting an experience.

Clairvoyance and Intuition

A simple definition for intuition is to reach a conclusion or thought without conscious reasoning or preceding thoughts. Supposed that before you leave your house and without seeing the weather forecast, the following idea comes to your mind: "you should take the umbrella." This could be the intuition that it will rain and, perhaps, at the end of the day, this information will prove useful when the rain starts.

Intuition normally happens spontaneously and usually does not involve images. It feels like the thought "surfaced" in your mind, or a sudden certainty about something, but without having thought about that subject, and without reaching that mental "place" with your own thoughts and reasoning.

The mechanism is important in this case. Clairvoyance is the visual perception of an external reality, in the present. Intuition, on the other hand, is an internal process, where you obtain information or reach a conclusion without the usual method of perceiving and reasoning.

Clairvoyance, Imagination, and Visualization

As discussed in the chapter "Perception of Images," there is a conscious effort – or will command – to generate the image in front of you.

The key difference is once more in the mechanism: clairvoyance is a mode of *perception*, and visualization/imagination is a form of *manifestation*. This is to say that the image that reaches us during clairvoyance is coming from the world *to us*. In a visualization and in our imagination we *create* the image, in other words, the process is the opposite, going *from us* to the image.

If I ask you to imagine a grape juice stain on this page of the book, you could easily close your eyes, remember the page of the book on your mental screen, then add the stain to the image. You could go further and visualize the glass with juice and how it got spilled on the book, the effect of the spillage on other pages, the exact shape of the stain, and details of the edge where the stain ends.

A bit more effort is needed in order to imagine the same stain with your eyes open, mainly because your eyes are constantly evidencing that the page is *not* stained. Still, with a bit of effort, you could visualize the stain, which would be the result of combining the imaginary stain with the real page you are seeing. You would not be "seeing" the stain with the intensity of a real stain; however, as long as your effort to create the stain is there, the stain will be there.

The key aspect of this example is "as long as your effort to create the stain is there." If you have your eyes open and passively observe the page, without the effort of imagining anything, the page will show as it is, without a stain.

It is a good idea to try the visualization and contrast it with the passive observation a few times, and to pay attention to how you are operating *internally* while you visualize the stain, to perceive the effort and will command you are issuing.

Being aware of the difference between passive observation and active visualization can help us answer the following question: *How do I know if I am not imagining the aura, energies, or the extraphysical consciousness that I am seeing?*

If you are you applying effort to imagine those elements, for example, if you are **actively** imagining an aura around the person you are looking at, then what you "see" could be the result of your imagination. If, however, during a **passive** observation, you see this aura, even for a brief period, then what you have seen is not imagination.

In normal conditions of health and lucidity there is no imagination without mental effort. To **see** an aura, an extraphysical consciousness, or extraphysical energies is one thing, to **imagine or visualize** is another. The difference is as clear as to drink water and to imagine yourself drinking water.

If you see this as a conundrum, removing all expectations while you apply a clairvoyance technique can help a lot. Expectations can make it harder for you to be in a quieter frame of mind and achieve a truly passive observation. The same goes for anxiety: reaching a serene psychosomatic state will help you detect the input of paravision and be more certain about it.

Ideally, we should try to act as a researcher during data collection. Or like a field ornithology researcher, to be precise. If you are trying to understand the behavior of a bird in its habitat, you will have to be *very* quiet during the observation, and concentrate on acquiring and recording everything you see. When you are back in your lab, you can move and make as much noise as you want while analyzing the data collected.

What happens quite often, especially in the beginning, when the clairvoyance perception is more subtle, is that doubts end up contributing to the confusion between perception and imagination. The expectation of a parapsychic "show" can contribute to this tendency.

Another element of complexity is if the experimenter is trying to maintain a certain image, or worries about what others will think if she does not see anything. An experimenter can find it hard to say, "I did not see any faces," during a group exercise when worried about people thinking, "He has been trying for so long, and still, nothing!" The pressure of the "public performance" could tempt this experimenter to classify anything as facial clairvoyance, even "editing" or "embellishing" her recall of the experiment, especially when many around her have reported perceptions.

With a bit of persistence in repeating exercises, perceptions will become more clear, to the point where the experimenter cannot deny those and be coherent with his own perceptions.

Clairvoyance and Retrocognitions

A retrocognition is a phenomenon where the consciousness becomes aware of facts, scenes, forms, objects, events, and experiences belonging to a previous life or to a period between lives. Retrocognition is popularly known as past life recall and the information we access during the phenomenon comes from our holomemory – an integral memory that aggregates all memories from all lives and all periods between lives. We can also have a retrocognition when we are out of the body, during a projection.

Retrocognition is a complex and interesting phenomenon that can be experienced in different ways and that can involve multiple parapsychic phenomena – including clairvoyance. Several conscientiology researchers point out that facial clairvoyance and retrocognition are interrelated.

The experience frequently includes scenes from a period prior to the current life "played" in front of the experimenter. At times, the scenes play out on a screen. In some cases, the experimenter feels immersed in the scene, and observes his own past self, as a spectator, as the scene unfolds. The experience can also present a blend between physical perception and access to holomemory.

An example of perception combining past and present was a retrocognition I had as I entered an Italian restaurant, in a neighborhood where many Italian descendants and immigrants lived.

The retrocognition happened on a night when some politician was hosting a dinner as part of his campaign. The "atmosphere" and energies of the place were probably part of the retrocognitive trigger.

Upon entering the restaurant, I saw two waiters walking quickly towards one another, about ten yards from where I was. As they passed each other and kept walking, something triggered a retrocognition and I had access to my holomemory. This access was presented over my normal physical vision: I could see that the restaurant decoration the clothing and people were different, as if I was in an Italian restaurant in the beginning of the 18th century. Some elements I could see, however, the faces of people near me as an example, were still from the present.

Although I know it was 1994, the images and energies were clearly from this prior epoch. Everything happened as if in slow motion. I heard music during the experience that I later noticed was not playing in the present. The restaurant general layout and table disposition remained more or less the same, suggesting the visual *input* from the present. The experience lasted a few seconds only, but brought a very strong energetic impact.

I needed a few minutes to recover from this impact, as the energies were clearly different and produced a sensation very different from the energies of the present life. It was clear to me that I was identifying a situation very similar to one I had experienced in a previous life, and the sensation was that I was practically living it again.

The energetic impact aspect might be the most important way to differentiate a retrocognition from clairvoyance or from other phenomena. A retrocognition comes with an impact because you identify that what you are seeing is part of *your* past.

Although the "vehicle" of clairvoyance and retrocognitions can be similar, to the extent that both contain images and visual aspects, the source of the images seen is very different. Clairvoyance brings images from the present (perception), while retrocognition images come from the past (holomemory).

Clairvoyance and Precognitions

A participant of one of the workshops, John, shared the following precognition account: As he sat down and relaxed during a pause at work, in a silent environment, a screen of about twenty inches "popped up" in front of him. The screen was about ten inches from his nose and he saw a "video" of about ten seconds where his brother met a common childhood friend in a park in Miami.

John discounted the possibility of travelling clairvoyance as he knew that during the experience his brother was in Columbia, South Carolina, and not walking in a park in Miami. John called his brother and confirmed that he was, indeed, in Columbia. As for the childhood friend, John had lost contact with him for approximately eight years, although there was a chance he could be living in Miami.

Three weeks later, John's brother came to spend a week in Miami. At that point, John had already forgotten about the experience that would later be confirmed as a precognition. During a morning run, his brother indeed met the childhood friend in the exact spot of the park seen in John's mental screen.

In this case the experience was not clairvoyance because the contents were not from something happening in the *present*. Instead, we classify the phenomenon as precognition because John was able to access what was likely to happen in the *future*.

We cannot always verify if what was observed is a precognition, as was the case in this example: John was able to call his brother right after the experience. We have to rely on other characteristics of the phenomenon when we cannot immediately verify information derived from it.

For example, a precognition often comes with a feeling that "this is something that *will* happen." In other words, the experimenter knows that the information pertains to the future.

Generally speaking, precognition events have a short duration, at times coming in a flash, a series of static images, or a scene played out in the experimenter's screen that lasts less than a minute.

While the images are playing, the experimenter can enter a type of trance where he cannot control certain aspects of the experience, for example, the angle of observation. More often than not the experimenter is unable to interrupt the experience. Both aspects are in sharp contrast with travelling clairvoyance, where the experimenter typically controls where he is looking and can terminate the phenomenon at will.

What Clairvoyance is Not

Some perceptions can clearly be identified as not being rooted in paravision. One example is when the experimenter sees in double, as in the account below:

I saw two copies of you, about 20 inches apart.

[Instructor]: What do you mean, two exact copies of me?

Yes. I could see you at the center [of my visual field, when we started the exercise] and, next, I started to see two copies pulling apart, slowly, one to the right, one to the left, up to the point they were completely separate, each about 10 inches from the [initial] central point.

[Instructor]: Did you see the whole body?

Yes, the whole body and the chair you were sitting on.

This perception can be explained in terms of changes in the convergence of the experimenter's physical eyes. In this case, the experimenter was about five yards away from the instructor. With relaxation and eyes open, the convergence changed from the central point and started to diverge. In other words, the muscles of the eyes relaxed and instead of pointing slightly inwards, they started to move outwards, towards a point where the line of sight of each eye was parallel to one another. The physical movement makes the effect of seeing two instructors, one for each eye.

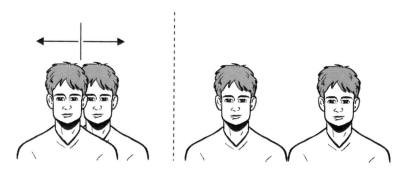

Figure 23: Double Image

Normally, a bit of practice is required in order to prevent this double image effect. It is necessary to train a "selective" relaxation of the soma, and stay in control of the muscles that control the direction of our eyesight. This is the same ability we use when we deeply relax our physical body while sitting, to the point we feel it almost floating, and yet manage keep the head straight and eyes open.

Optical illusions are another example of something that is not clairvoyance. Some optical illusions can be used as a "bridge" technique to reach clairvoyance, or simply to learn how to observe new aspects of physical vision. And as explored in the topic "Finding the Switch" in Chapter 6, new experiences and identification of subtleties are helpful in clairvoyance.

Chapter 10

Conclusions

The Clairvoyance Workshop, a substantial source of information for this book, has changed significantly since its original version. New explanations, examples and, in some cases, variations of exercises were added along the way, as those were repeated with different groups of people.

I expect the same for future editions of this book: an evolving set of techniques and theories based on personal experience, accounts from experimenters, theoretical research, reflection, and practical experiments.

This chapter presents partial conclusions about a few clairvoyance aspects. Naturally, the conclusions presented here are not definitive nor absolute. Theories, methods, and techniques are relative truths, applied until new hypotheses surface and reach a relative consensus among researchers.

Overcoming Exaggerated Skepticism and Self-Blocking

The second time Bruce participated in a workshop, he presented the following question:

I have an issue: every time I start to see the energosoma of the instructor I start to wonder if this is some sort of optical illusion or effect of the illumination. How can I work this out?

Based on experience, the answer that helps the most involves two strategies: (a) increase the difference and (b) leave analysis for later.

The "increase the difference" consists of training more; try more times and with different techniques, to achieve experiences that leave no doubt to the experimenter.

No experience will change the experimenter if he decides to cling to a physicalist paradigm, of course. We already discussed the case where the person unconsciously sabotages his own efforts and classifies any experience as irrelevant or inconclusive. It is possible, however, and I venture to say it is also relatively simple, to increase the contrast between physical and extra-physical perception to the point a lucid and rational experimenter will not be able to deny it.

We can use the exercise where we try to see someone else's energosoma as an example. If I see a bright outline that is **half an inch** thick, perhaps I could discount it as an illusion that stems from the natural functioning my physical eyes. I can try to explain it based on retinal persistence, how my brain processes edge detection in low light conditions, or something along those lines.

If I see an outline of **two or three inches**, clearly different from the outline I am seeing around a piece of furniture, and this outline around the person I am looking at appears alive, with strong brightness, I have to admit that such perception does not fit into any physical explanation.

As per "leaving analysis for later," this is something that was discussed in the Chapter 6, on the section "Self-blocking." In summary, the principle is to avoid questioning and analysis *during* the clairvoyance exercise, since this mental attitude could block our paraperceptions. If you are relaxed, with the spirit of an explorer, open to new perceptions, and not concerned with consequences and potential conclusions, you will allow clair-voyance to develop more easily. The critical analysis, as important as it is, can wait until after the experiment.

Clairvoyance as a Diagnostic Tool

I have seen the proposition of using clairvoyance as a diagnostic tool in many mystical fairs across countries like Brazil, United

States, Mexico, Portugal, and Spain.

Although clairvoyance can potentially be used as a complementary method for anamnesis, I have not yet seen, up to this moment, bibliography with detailed information and well-defined methodology, case studies or more formal research. This makes me think that there is a lot to be studied in this particular area.

Some books propose a system of evaluation and instructions to translate what we see in an aura in terms of health and illness. Those systems, however, are often conceived by *one* person, meaning the validation by others is missing. A more complete research report would require consensus in terms of language and validation through common experiences.

This is not to diminish the merit of several pioneers in terms of clairvoyance anamnesis. In the current context, however, a checkup based on conventional medicine would probably produce a more exact diagnostic, especially when trying to assess the health of the physical body.

A conventional exam would be restricted to the physical body, of course, and would miss the blockage of a chakra, for example. Nevertheless, even for an issue that is not somatic, it is probably more productive to learn how to perceive your own energy body and unblocking your chakras through individual energy work.

We could receive help from someone else to identify and eliminate problems in our energosoma, and perhaps this would be something helpful in a minority of cases. To lean on external help for everything, as a standard conduct, would be equivalent to eating lots of sugar, trans fats, and deep-fried foods all your life and trust that any heart issues will be resolved by a good cardiologist.

Subjective Phenomena and Manipulation
A very common question I hear is "How is my aura?" The answer I offer, and chosen as a personal principle, is "Develop your clair-

voyance and look in the mirror." I chose this answer in an attempt to break the culture of "outsourcing" spirituality or psychic experiences, a culture that often keeps people stuck in past life repetition or in a state of reduced individual responsibility towards her own energies.

Other potential problems in evaluating another person through paraperceptions are manipulation, seduction, and psychological dependencies. Suppose someone hears the following from a supposed psychic person:

"Your aura is very strong... You must be an advanced spirit... The color, violet... You are a spirit of light..."

This person will certainly be tempted to believe in the subjective perception of the psychic, especially because there is praise included in the perception. The bigger the ego of the listener, the higher the probability to believe in this diagnostic, even if it is false or no personal evidence is available to back the assessment.

Diagnosis from third parties, therefore, can be used for manipulation when the parapsychic is lacking ethics – or, in this case, *cosmo*ethics.

Another example I heard in a mystical fair could have a hidden motive of creating some sort of dependency:

"Mmmm, the aura is not closed properly... There is not a lot of light... I see dark colors around the abdomen... This chakra must be blocked, there must be an issue there..."

A great number of people would find it hard to dismiss this comment and would be curious to hear more about the "problem" and how to solve it. Let us put aside, temporarily, the discussion about the validity of the diagnostic. We will discuss this a bit later. If the identification of the problem was offered by the parapsychic-clairvoyant, it would be natural to believe that the same person could have a solution to that particular problem and perhaps, to many other problems. The intersubjective nature of the interaction can create a pathological dependency depending on the level of ethics and personality of those involved.

There is the possibility of conflicts of interest in this intersubjective interaction. A psychic person that has financial interests to defend, for being heavily dependent on the activity to pay her own personal bills, or to build personal wealth, for example, could be faced with choosing between an approach that helps those involved, and an approach that maximizes profit.

Additionally, there are complex ramifications of the relationship between the psychic person and the non-psychic person that could result in a guru-follower pattern: the guru supposedly has exclusive access to other dimensions, and thinks and makes decisions *for* the follower. The dependency could place the follower at a disadvantage in terms of personal development, mentalsoma, discernment, omni-questioning, and rationality.

Mabel Teles, in her book *Prophylaxis of Consciential Manipulation* (in Portuguese: *Profilaxia das Manipulações Conscienciais*), summarizes this aspect with the following sentence: "He who takes, in practice and with lucidity, the reins of his own conduct and evolution, minimizes the possibility of being an intraphysical consciousness subject to manipulation."

Outsourcing the Experience of Other Dimensions

One of conscientiology propositions is to prioritize individual parapsychic development to increase the frequency and quality of direct experiences with multidimensionality.

Ideally, an experimenter should seek personal validation of any third-party perception and vice-versa. I would then verify my perceptions with others and others would verify their perceptions with me. As an example, if I had seen a blue aura in an oval shape, I would ask another experimenter if this is what she has seen. This simple procedure can help in consensus building and, little by little, in understanding more about the phenomenon.

For the validation of perceptions to work, it is necessary for the participants to have common language to describe the phenomenon, and a more or less equalized level of discernment and parapsychic perception capacity.

It will not always be possible to validate our perceptions with third parties, as others may have different perceptions or, at times, we may have a spontaneous phenomenon when no one is around. Additionally, we cannot expect that the interpretation of the paraperceptions will always be the same in a group, all the time. Despite such complexities, the initiative to seek for practical experience and communication will definitely help to achieve a mature and independent parapsychic ability.

In group experiments, the profile of the participants matters. If three out of five are more mystical and have a tendency to talk about extraterrestrials 90 percent of the time, the group could have the attention more focused on this kind of perception and exclude anything outside this theme.

If the other two participants feel "out of place" and react by seeking approval from the majority, they could end up agreeing and validating the perception of others by, for example, nodding along even when their perceptions contradict what the majority has seen.

A concept I learned in a type of activity called "dynamics" at CEAEC, is called "parapsychic de-repression." The concept involves saying what you have perceived regardless of what you think about it, even when you think it is absurd, and regardless of what others might think about it. At first, an experimenter tends mix everything: imagination, free association, and guesswork with parapsychic perception. After many months of weekly exercise, along with an element of objective verification that is included in most dynamics, and the validation (or not) based on observations from others in the group, the experimenter gains confidence in his own parapsychic ability and learns how to separate what is parapsychism from what is not.

In the context of group experiments it is also important to understand that the holothosene of the group determines the quality of the field of energies established, and the type of extraphysical consciousness that will be attracted by that field. If a certain number of people adopt a religious approach, consciously or not, or believe in angels, or favors the consolation approach, or a more emotional approach, the extraphysical consciousnesses that participate will tend to have an energy pattern that is more consolation-oriented and maternal/paternal.

To be closer to multidimensional *reality*, it is indispensable to associate parapsychic development to consciential development, always based on self-scrutiny and self-knowledge.

Effective Alternative Therapies

Prioritizing personal experiences does not mean discarding energetic interventions from third parties as effective therapies. Both personal experience and scientific experiments bring evidence that, in specific conditions, the extraphysical energy work can help as a complement to conventional types of therapy.

What is essential is to keep your eyes and *para*eyes open, with your discernment switched on to identify what is more intelligent, a higher priority, important for personal growth and to help others. The more you know about the subject and the more you have personal experiences, the better.

A Long Road Ahead

Extraphysical Vision is a very rich phenomenon. It is also quite complex at times. There is a lot of work to be done in order to thoroughly understand this phenomenon, especially in terms of organization and consensus around paravision perceptions and correlation. There are loads of hypotheses to be more formally validated and specific methods and techniques for research can be more clearly defined.

If you would like to contribute with your experience for clairvoyance research, you will find a survey on http://www.clairvoyancebook.com/survey.

Steps toward Self-Knowledge

As pointed out in this book, clairvoyance is an accessible phenomenon that can bring a number of benefits and deep, extraordinary parapsychic experiences.

Each person will need to work on a different set of skills to develop this ability to its fullest. The first step is to find the switch, something mainly related to relaxation and bioenergies. The second step is to learn how to change your clairvoyance tuning at will. You can achieve this by adding active clairvoyance techniques to your experimentation program. The moment that you learn how to operate this "channel-changing" switch, you will have a valuable tool to increase your experience set.

Developing the ability to access extraphysical dimensions without mysticisms or indoctrinations is an important aspect of evolutionary intelligence: it enables us to get the most out of our experiences.

We also explored why clairvoyance represents a tip of the metaphorical (very interesting) iceberg. It could help us to address the question "what are we doing in this world?"

If you have reached this page after reading this book, it is probable that you do not subscribe to the theory that the physical world is all that is. To believe in this and align with the "consensus trance" of society is relatively easy, but unnecessary.

The proposition is that, through clairvoyance development, you experience other dimensions and, from there, get further motivated to develop other forms of parapsychism. This will open a new array of possibilities in the exploration of reality around you, and of your own reality as a multidimensional consciousness.

Enjoy your experiences!

Acknowledgements

I am thankful for many people I have interacted with in this life. For this particular project, a big thank you goes to the participants of the clairvoyance workshops and parapsychic development classes, who contributed so much with questions, accounts, and insights. A big thanks to all volunteers that organized, promoted, and made all those workshops possible. Special mention goes to "the crew" from Florida in particular – for the companionship and good times while working shoulder to shoulder. Then, for the often not detected, extraphysical helpers that supported those activities.

I am particularly grateful to Patricia Sousa, evolutionary duo, wife, love of my life, and partner in consciential endeavors, who offered constant support. Her ideas, criticism and central role in organizing workshops, courses, meetings, and trips were essential for this project. You are inspiration and happiness, strength and determination, how great to have met you once more, in this life.

I want to thank Katia Arakaki and Graça Razera for valuable support as I was starting to write, and the many volunteer-proof-readers from several organizations linked to conscientiology. Thank you Ulisses, the Editor of the first edition in Portuguese, for all the work during the copyediting phase, thoughtfulness, and appreciation to the approach chosen for this book. Many thanks to Liliana Alexandre, for the enthusiastic support for the English edition.

Special thanks to Waldo Vieira, for creating a theoretical-practical framework for the study of consciousness, for his insights, for teaching that "there are no horizons," for motivating me to apply rationality while going beyond the physical dimension, for the welcoming approach, and for patient support while I developed my understanding of conscientiology.

I want to thank my father, Romero, for reading the whole book, wholeheartedly and with an open mind, for the feedback, and for reporting his own experiences after reading the book. To my mother, Marlene, for the wisdom and sharpness in all observations. Rafael, Aline, Yole and Leila, who, in a way or another, were great companions with whom I learned a lot, in many ways and various situations. To Rogério, great father-in-law, for the critical review, conversations, and ideas presented. Also thanks to my aunt Elvira, for the principles of self-overcoming presented at the right time in this life.

Rodrigo Medeiros
London, October 2016

From the Author

Thank you for your interest in *Paravision: Theory and Practice of Visual Clairvoyance.* If you liked this book, please leave your comments on your favorite bookseller site. Please visit www.clairvoyancebook.org for the latest blog posts, to contribute by participating on a survey, view survey results, read articles, connect with people interested in psychic development and consciousness development, or to sign up to our newsletter.

Annex I: About Conscientiology and Cognopolis

Cognopolis (City of Knowledge) is a suburb created in 2009 in the city of Foz do Iguaçu, Parana, Brazil, where 25 organizations focused on consciousness studies operate, based on the work of volunteers. Constituted by city ordinance 18887, Cognopolis has green spaces with walking trails, residential condominiums, the Mabu Interludium Hotel, and activities related to education, culture, and research.

Also known as the Suburb of Volunteering, Cognopolis was conceived by the professor, lexicographer, and doctor, Waldo Vieira (1932–2015).

The Holocycle is a fundamental component of Cognopolis and a site of conscientiology intellectual production. The name is a composition of the word "holo," meaning "set," and the "cycle," a segment from the word "encyclopedia." Considered an incubator of authors, it contains one of the largest lexicothecas (collections of dictionaries) in Brazil, with more than 6,800 items, an encyclotheca (a collection of encyclopedias), and a newspaper and magazine clippings library with more than 570,000 clippings.

The Holotheca (a set of thecas, or collections) is also part of cognopolis and contains approximately 873,011 items, of which 96,911 are books and other written materials. There are also collections of objects from several places and cultures. The comic book theca, a collection of comic books, is considered to be one of the largest in Latin America, as it contains over 35,000 comic books published in 16 languages from 22 countries.

Scientific events are frequently held in Cognopolis to disseminate research results and stimulate debate. Writing books and articles is also strongly encouraged in the City of knowledge. Among the 841 volunteers, 119 are published authors, of which 78 wrote on conscientiology topics.

Cognopolis is open to visitors and is a part of Foz do Iguaçu's tourist route.

For more information, please contact CEAEC:

Website: www.ceaec.org
Facebook: Campus CEAEC
E-mail: ceaec@ceaec.org

Annex II: About Waldo Vieira

Waldo Vieira was born in April 12, 1932 in Monte Carmelo, Minas Gerais, Brazil, and passed away on July 2, 2015 in Foz do Iguaçu, Brazil, where he lived since the year 2000.

A graduate in Medicine and Dentistry and the proposer of the sciences Projectiology and Conscientiology, which he systematized in the treatises *Projectiology: A Panorama of Experiences of the Consciousness Outside the Human Body* (1986), and *700 Conscientiology Experiments* (1994).

He created the suburb called Cognopolis (City of Knowledge) in Foz do Iguaçu, where he taught daily Conscientiological Tertulias, from 2002 to 2014, and conscientiological minitertulias from 2013 to 2015, in the Tertuliarium at the Centre for Higher Studies of Conscientiology (CEAEC).

Vieira also conceived and structured the Holotheca, through the donation of his personal library on the subjects of consciousness and the out-of-body experience, and the Holocycle, an environment specializing in lexicography, where he coordinated research teams that developed the Encyclopedia of Conscientiology, of which he was the creator, organizer, and author of 2019 entries.

Vieira was cited in the British publication *Who's Who in the 21st Century*, a book published by the IBC – International Biographical Centre. He is the author of 25 books on the subject of conscientiology, including treatises and lexicons.

References

The references below include several types of books with a wide range of approaches, from the very materialistic ones to some very mystical.

Several of the books that were consulted offered ideas and definitions that were in contradiction and, at times, ideas that are opposite of what was presented in this book. Because of that, the references are divided into three sections: conscientiological bibliography, general bibliography, and mystical bibliography.

We cannot say that there is an absolute consensus across all conscientiological books, as it is a relatively "young" and dynamic science. However, the fundamental concepts and the paradigm utilized in the conscientiological references are uniform. This makes the understanding of certain topics discussed in this book easier, should you choose to read more about, for example, cosmoethics and helpers.

The general bibliography, mostly related to clairvoyance and physical visual perception, presents useful information, although not all approaches are aligned to those presented in this book, and a few of those books present some traces of mysticism.

The third section, mystical bibliography, is the one that requires the most amount of "filtering" since, from my perspective, the majority of these books are strongly influenced by occultism, religions, and esoteric movements. Those works present approaches at times outdated, at times counterproductive and/or confusing, and, at times, simply without a broader validation. In spite of that, the titles presented contain cases, examples, techniques, and ideas that can be useful when contributing to the development of the research approach proposed here.

Conscientiological Bibliography

Balona, Málu. *Síndrome do Estrangeiro* (Rio de Janeiro: Instituto Internacional de Projeciologia e Conscienciologia [IIPC], 1998)

Buonato, Flávio & **Zolet**, Lilian. *Manual do Acoplamentarium* (Foz do Iguaçu, Brazil: Editares, 2014)

Cirera, Miguel. *Evolución de la Inteligência Parapsiquica* (Foz do Iguaçu, Brazil: Editares, 2014)

Daou, Dulce. *Autoconsciência e Multidimensionalidade* (Foz do Iguaçu, Brazil: Editares, 2005)

Gonçalves, Moacir & **Salles**, Rosemary. *Dinâmicas Parapsíquicas* (Foz do Iguaçu, Brazil: Editares, 2013)

Gustus, Sandie. *Less Incomplete: A Guide to Experiencing the Human Condition beyond the Physical Body* (London: 6th Books, 2011)

Lutfi, Lucy. *Voltei para Contar. Autobiografia de uma Experimentadora da Quase-Morte* (Foz do Iguaçu, Brazil: Editares, 2006)

Medeiros, Rodrigo & **Sousa**, Patricia. *Image Target Research Project: a methodology to support research on remote perception phenomena* (New York: Proceedings of the III ICPC – International Congress of Projectiology and Conscientiology, 2002)

Schlosser, Ulisses. *Técnica para o Ajustamento Parafisiológico da Sintonia Visual na Clarividência* (Foz do Iguaçu, Brazil: CEAEC Editora, Article, *Revista Conscientia*. V. 11, N. 3, 2007.)

Teles, Mabel. *Profilaxia das Manipulações Conscienciais* (Foz do Iguaçu, Brazil: Editares 2007)

Vieira, Waldo. *200 Teáticas da Conscienciologia* (Rio de Janeiro: Instituto Internacional de Projeciologia e Conscienciologia [IIPC], 1997)

—, *700 Experimentos da Conscienciologia* (Rio de Janeiro: Instituto Internacional de Projeciologia e Conscienciologia [IIPC], 1994)

—, *Homo sapiens reurbanisatus* (Foz do Iguaçu, Brazil: CEAEC Editora, 2003)

—, *Homo sapiens pacificus* (Foz do Iguaçu, Brazil: CEAEC Editora, 2007)

—, *Our Evolution* (Foz do Iguaçu, Brazil: Editares, 2016)

—, *Projectiology: a panorama of experiences of the consciousness outside the human body* (New York, USA: International Institute of Projectiology and Conscientiology [IIPC], 2002)

—, *Projections of the Consciousness* (New York, USA: International Institute of Projectiology and Conscientiology, – IIPC, 1997.

Zolet, Lilian & **Kunz**, Guilherme. *Acoplamentarium: Primeira Década* (Foz do Iguaçu, Brazil: Editares, 2013)

General Bibliography

Bagnal, Oscar. *The Origins and Properties of the Human Aura* (New York: University Books, 1974)

Bodycombe, David J. *Optical Illusions and Picture Puzzles* (New York: Barnes and Noble Books, 1999)

Butler, W.E. *How to Read the Aura. Its Character and Function in Everyday Life* (Wellingborough, UK: The Aquarian Press, 1979) —, *How to Read the Aura, Practice Psychometry, Telepathy and Clairvoyance* (New York: Destiny Books, 1978)

Carrington, Hereward. *The Problems of Psychical Research* (Charleston, SC, USA: 1921 Edition Reprint, Bibliobazaar, 2008

Petit Dictionaire Anglais Francais (Paris: Hachette, 1934)

Dixon, Jacob. *Hygienic Clairvoyance* (London: W. Foulsham & Co, 1920)

Felton, Russell. *My Passport Says Clairvoyant* (New York: Hawthorn Books Inc., 1974)

Fonseca, José. *Novo Dicionário Lello. Francês Português* (Porto: Lello, 1997)

Geley, Gustave. *Clairvoyance and Materialisation: a Record of Experiments* (London: Bouverie House, 1927)

IANDS. *The Day I Died: The Mind, the Brain, and Near-Death Experiences* (Produced by British Broadcasting Company [BBC]; Distributed by Films for the Humanities and Sciences, 2002)

Johnson, R.C. *Psychical Research* (London: English Universities Press, 1923)

Jones, Zachary; **Dunne**, Brenda; **Jahn**, Robert and **Hoeger**, Elissa. *Filters and Reflections: Perspectives on Reality* (Princeton, NJ: ICRL Press, 2009)

Kitaoka, Akiyoshi & **Ashida,** Hiroshi. *Phenomenal Characteristics of the Periferal Drift Illusion* (Kyoto: Journal of the Vision Society of Japan, 2003)

Lomel, van Pim. *Consciousness Beyond Life* (London: Harper Collins, 2010)

Marleau-Ponty, Maurice. *Fenomenologia da Percepção* (São Paulo, Brazil: LMFE, 1999)

McConnell, R.A. *Self Deception in Science* (Pittsburgh: University of Pittsburgh, 1982)

McMoneagle, Joseph. *Mind Trek: Exploring Consciousness, Time, and Space Through Remote Viewing*, (Charlottesville, Virginia: Hampton Roads, 1997)

—, *Remote Viewing Secrets: a Handbook* (Charlottesville: Hampton Roads, 2000)

—, *The Ultimate Time Machine: A Remote Viewer's Perception of Time, and Predictions for the New Millenium* (Charlottesville, Virginia: Hampton Roads, 1998.

Melville, John. *The Wonders of Crystal Gazing and Clairvoyance* (London: W. Foulsham & Co Ltd., 1920)

Meyer, Philippe. *O Olho e o Cérebro: Biofilosofia da Percepção Visual* (São Paulo: Editora UNESP, 1997)

Oppenheim, Janet. *The Other World: Spiritualism and Psychical Research in England* (Cambridge: Cambridge University Press, 1985)

Osborne, Gladys L. *My Life in Two Worlds* (London: Cassell & Company Ltd., 1931)

Owens, Elizabeth. *Spiritualism & Clairvoyance for Beginners* (Woodbury, MN, USA: First Edition. Llewellyn Publications, 2007)

Ring, Kenneth & **Cooper**, Sharon. *Mindsight. Near-Death and Out-of-Body Experiences in the Blind* (Palo Alto, USA: William James Center for Consciousness Studies, 1999)

Rock, Irvin. *Perception* (New York: Scientific American Books, 1984)

Santaella, Lucia. *Semiótica Aplicada* (São Paulo: Pioneira Thomson Learning, 2005)

Smith, Angela Thompson. *Remote Perceptions: Out-Of-Body*

Experiences, Remote Viewing, and Other Normal Abilities; Foreword by Ingo Swan (Charlottesville; Virginia: Hampton Roads, 1998)

Smith, Mark. *Auras: See Them in Only 60 Seconds!* (St. Paul, Minnesota: Llewellyn Publications, 2002)

Smith, Paul H. *Reading the Enemy's Mind: Inside Stargate – America's Psychic Espionage Program* (New York: Tom Doherty Associates, 2006)

Silva, Roberto Epifânio da & **Silva,** Ilza Andrade. *O Plano Extrafísico. Pesquisa através da Clarividência* (Londrina, Brazil: Livraria e Editora Universalista, 1997)

Tart, Charles. *Body, Mind, Spirit. Exploring the Parapsychology of Spirituality* (Charlottesville, Virginia: Hampton Roads, 1997)

Wallace, Alfred Russell. *O Aspecto Científico do Sobrenatural* (Niterói, Brazil: Lachâtre, 2003)

Wasielewski, Dr. Waldemar. *Telepatia, Visión Hipnótica y Clarividência: Facultades Psíquicas Extraordinárias* (Barcelona, Spain: Casa Editorial Mauci, 1921)

Mystical Bibliography

Andrews, Ted. *How to See and Read the Aura* (St. Paul, Minnesota: Llewellyn, 2002)

Besant, A. & **Leadbeater,** C.W. *Formas de Pensamento: 27 Pranchas em Cores* (São Paulo, Brazil: Pensamento, Original Edition in1901)

Bierce, Ambrose. *The Enlarged Devil's Dictionary* (London: Penguin Books, 1971, p. 70)

Cayce, Edgar. *Auras: an Essay on the Meaning of Colors* (Virginia Beach, VA, USA: A.R.E. Press, 48th Printing from original essay in 1945, 2008)

Fiorentin, Arlindo; *A Abertura do Terceiro Olho: a Visão Psíquica* (São Paulo, Brazil: Ediouro, 1986)

Hemser, Gloria & **Friedlander,** John. *Desenvolvimento Psíquico Básico: Aura, Chakras e Clarividência* (São Paulo, Brazil; Pensamento, 1999)

Kilner, Walter J. *The Human Aura* (Seacaucis, New Jersey: Citadel Press, 1965)

Leadbeater, C. W. *Clarividencia. La Percepción de los Mundos Invisibles* (Barcelona, Spain: Ediciones Abraxas, 1999)
—, *Man Visible and Invisible: Examples of Different Types of Men as seen by Means of Trained Clairvoyance* (London: The Teosophical Publishing House, 1969)
—, *O Homem Visível e Invisível: um Estudo das Variações da Aura dos Diferentes Tipos de Indivíduos* (São Paulo: Pensamento, 1987)

Lewis, Ralph M. *A Través Del Ojo de la Mente* (San José: Gran Logia Suprema de AMORC, 1983)

Maffucci, Maria. *L'aura-soma. Colori per Il Corpo, Colori per lo Spirito* (Milano: Xênia, 2005)

Mala, Matthias. *A Aura das Mãos. O Significado das Cores e das Formas da Aura* (São Paulo, Brazil: Pensamento, 1993)

Oso, Jiménez Del. *El Sexto Sentido, los Ojos de la Mente* (Mexico City, Mexico: Universo, 1982)

Ouseley, S. **Fortune,** Dion & **de la Fleuriere,** Raoul. *El Aura Humana* (Mexico City, Mexico: Queipo Hnos, Editores *S. de R.L.*)

Schnabel, Jim. *Remote Viewers: The Secret History of America's Psychic Spies* (New York: Dell Publishing, 1997)

Shumsky, Susan G. *Exploring Auras. Cleansing and Strengthening Your Energy Field* (Franklin Lakes, NJ: New Page Books, 2006)

Slate, Joe H. *Aura Energy for Health, Healing and Balance* (Woodsbury, Minessotta: Llewellyn Publications, 1999)

Spencer, Wolfran R. *Clarividência, Telepatia y Parapsicologia* (Mexico City, Mexico: Editores, Mexicanos Unidos, 1996)

Spilmont, Jean-Pierre. *A Vidência* (São Paulo, Brazil: Martins Fontes Editora, 1983)

Vishita, Swami Bhakta. *The Development of Seership, the Science of Knowing the Future. Hindoo and Oriental Methods* (Chicago: The Yogi Publication Society, 1960)

Webster, Richard. *Aura Reading for Beginners. Develop your Psychic Awareness for Health and Success* (St. Paul, Minessota: Llewellyn Publications, 2003)

Wikinski, Bernardo. *Aura, los Extraordinários Atributos de Nuestra Energia* (Buenos Aires: Kier, 2004)

Field of Research

Paraperceptiology, a subspecialty of Conscientiology

6th Books

ALL THINGS PARANORMAL

Investigations, explanations and deliberations on the
paranormal, supernatural, explainable or unexplainable. 6th
Books seeks to give answers while nourishing the soul: whether
making use of the scientific model or anecdotal and fun, but
always beautifully written.
Titles cover everything within parapsychology: how to,
lifestyles, alternative medicine, beliefs, myths and theories.
If you have enjoyed this book, why not tell other readers by
posting a review on your preferred book site? Recent
bestsellers from 6th Books are:

The Afterlife Unveiled
What the Dead Are Telling us About Their World!
Stafford Betty
What happens after we die? Spirits speaking through mediums
know, and they want us to know. This book unveils their
world...
Paperback: 978-1-84694-496-3 ebook: 978-1-84694-926-5

Spirit Release
Sue Allen
A guide to psychic attack, curses, witchcraft, spirit attachment,
possession, soul retrieval, haunting, deliverance, exorcism and
more, as taught at the College of Psychic Studies.
Paperback: 978-1-84694-033-0 ebook: 978-1-84694-651-6

I'm Still With You
True Stories of Healing Grief Through Spirit Communication
Carole J. Obley
A series of after-death spirit communications which uplift,
comfort and heal, and show how love helps us grieve.
Paperback: 978-1-84694-107-8 ebook: 978-1-84694-639-4

Advanced Psychic Development
Becky Walsh
Learn how to practise as a professional, contemporary spiritual
medium.
Paperback: 978-1-84694-062-0 ebook: 978-1-78099-941-8

Astral Projection Made Easy
Overcoming the Fear of Death
Stephanie June Sorrell
From the popular Made Easy series, Astral Projection Made
Easy helps to eliminate the fear of death, through discussion of
life beyond the physical body.
Paperback: 978-1-84694-611-0 ebook: 978-1-78099-225-9

The Miracle Workers Handbook
Seven Levels of Power and Manifestation of the Virgin Mary
Sherrie Dillard
Learn how to invoke the Virgin Mary's presence, communicate
with her, receive her grace and miracles and become a miracle
worker.
Paperback: 978-1-84694-920-3 ebook: 978-1-84694-921-0

Divine Guidance
The Answers You Need to Make Miracles
Stephanie J. King
Ask any question and the answer will be presented, like a direct line to higher realms... Divine Guidance helps you to regain control over your own journey through life.
Paperback: 978-1-78099-794-0 ebook: 978-1-78099-793-3

The End of Death
How Near-Death Experiences Prove the Afterlife
Admir Serrano
A compelling examination of the phenomena of Near-Death Experiences.
Paperback: 978-1-78279-233-8 ebook: 978-1-78279-232-1

Less Incomplete
A Guide to Experiencing the Human Condition Beyond the Physical Body
Sandie Gustus
Based on 40 years of scientific research, this book is a dynamic guide to understanding life beyond the physical body.
Paperback: 978-1-84694-351-5 ebook: 978-1-84694-892-3

The Psychic & Spiritual Awareness Manual
A Guide to DIY Enlightenment
Kevin West
Discover practical ways of empowering yourself by unlocking your psychic awareness, through the Spiritualist and New Age approach.
Paperback: 978-1-78279-397-7 ebook: 978-1-78279-396-0

Readers of ebooks can buy or view any of these bestsellers by clicking on the live link in the title. Most titles are published in paperback and as an ebook. Paperbacks are available in traditional bookshops. Both print and ebook formats are available online.

Find more titles and sign up to our readers' newsletter at http://www.johnhuntpublishing.com/mind-body-spirit. Follow us on Facebook at https://www.facebook.com/OBooks and Twitter at https://twitter.com/obooks.